NOT BY BREAD ALONE

NOT BY BREAD ALONE

Wheaton Chapel Talks

Compiled and Edited by

CARL F. H. HENRY

46364

ZONDERVAN PUBLISHING HOUSE

Grand Rapids, Michigan

TO THE WHEATON FAMILY EVERYWHERE
WHOSE FAITHFUL PRAYERS AND GRACIOUS
GIFTS HAVE MADE POSSIBLE A GREAT WORK
FOR CHRIST AND HIS KINGDOM

ACKNOWLEDGMENTS

Appreciation is expressed to those whose messages are in part reproduced in the pages of this book, and to Miss Joan Wise, of the College stenographic staff, for their fine spirit of coöperation.

PREFACE

From the spiritual leadership of the conservative Christian world come men renowned in the classroom, pulpit, and mission station, to bring to the Wheaton College chapel hour a cross-section of the religious fiber of the nations.

The Christian view of God and the world is pressed near to the heart of the Wheaton family—faculty, staff, and students—each class-day morning. Here is a veritable mountain-side where daily is enacted the feeding of the eleven hundred.

To many a conference hearing have come these same speakers, telling Christians how to live, how to serve, how to die. They preach one gospel: redemptive grace in Christ Jesus. They urge men to turn from materialistic subservience to the purpose and program of God.

"Not by bread alone!" plead pulpit orators such as Ironside, Houghton, Rimmer, Smith.

"Not by bread alone!" cry missionary standard-bearers such as Page, Scott, Bingham, Graham.

"Not by bread alone!" exhort theologians such as Thiessen, Koller, Walvoord.

"Not by bread alone!" assert professional and business men such as Wilson, Emory.

"Not by bread alone!" declare educators such as Buswell, Clark, Edman.

Such is the happy spirit of a Christian college. Scholarship and spirituality are not divorced but rather they are here the handmates of effective Christian service.

To the disciples, Jesus said, "Gather up the fragments that remain, that nothing be lost." This we have done. It is in that spirit that this volume comes to its reader audience.

It would be unfair to expect of any compiler that in the limits of so small a volume he shall express in full measure the spiritual feast set before the Wheaton family during the past year. It has been necessary to be selective. No message of the college year has been without blessing. Some, in God's providence, have been preparatory, working in needy hearts an attitude conducive to later response. So it is that God works, mysteriously, quietly, effectively, using the spiritual giants to whom the pulpit of Pierce Chapel is made available.

There is a trend at present to family reading at night. These epitomized chapel addresses, presented as nearly as possible in the words of the speakers, are published with the sincere prayer that God will bless them to the hearts of Wheaton friends. They will make excellent devotional reading, supplementing Bible study.

CARL F. H. HENRY

CONTENTS

8 *Contents*

THE BIBLE A LITERARY GEM —
AND MORE!

PREFERRING GOD'S WILL AT ANY COST

Since the second World War, a new term has come into use: "scuttling the ship."

Remember the story of the Graf Spee and the Columbus! How much more willing should we be to scuttle our ship than to have the enemy use it! If God has commanded you to set something aside, do it! If you do not, the evil one may use it against you.

Are you in the place where nothing matters but the will of God for your life? Would you be willing to scuttle the plans you have made? What about those pleasures, possibly things that have taken great hold on you? If they should be found things not pleasing to God, would you be willing to scuttle them? How about friendships that might not be in the plan of God for you?

The story of Abraham and Isaac is that of a man who was willing to go all the way with God, to do His will even when it meant sacrificing his son. God could say of Abraham, "There is a man who was willing to have My purpose carried out." Are you? Job is another who wanted God's will. He said, "The purposes of my heart are broken off." Are yours?

It is a wonderful thing to get to the place where we are cut off from everything in the world and stand alone with God.

THE REV. ADDISON RAWS,
Director of America's Keswick, Keswick Grove, N. J.

THE BIBLE A LITERARY GEM — AND MORE!

By Dr. Will H. Houghton, D. D.
President, Moody Bible Institute

> *Thy Word is like a garden, Lord,*
> *With flowers bright and fair;*
> *And everyone who seeks may pluck*
> *A lovely cluster there.*
> *Thy Word is like a deep, deep mine;*
> *And jewels rich and rare*
> *Are hidden in the mighty depths*
> *For every searcher there.*
>
> *Thy Word is like a starry host:*
> *A thousand rays of light*
> *Are seen to guide the traveler*
> *And make his pathway bright.*
> *Thy Word is like an armory,*
> *Where soldiers may repair*
> *And find, for life's long battle-day*
> *All needful weapons there.*

Boswell's Johnson once asked and answered: "Who is the most miserable man?"

"The man who can't read on a rainy day."

It had a good deal of truth in Dr. Johnson's time of serious writing and labored reading. But with the increase of filthy fiction and sexy pulp writings, the answer needs addition. The most unfortunate man is the man who reads the wrong thing. Oh, who will take the litter out of present-day literature? It clutters the news-stands and confuses the mind and darkens the character. Some fictionists use realism as a cloak for filth. They are the bats and buzzards of literature. Realism to a bat is darkness, and life to a buzzard is carrion. With the printing-presses grinding out books and periodicals, and with the many mortgages on time, the present-day reader must be highly selective lest his reading hours be harmful or at least wasted.

The old question, "what ten books would you take if you were to be shipwrecked on a lonely isle?" is perhaps more difficult to answer now than ever, but the chances are fair that most of your books would date back beyond the modern list. After all, the lonely isle test is not mere reading but rereading. Where in all earth's libraries is there a book for rereading like the Bible? Inexhaustible in its wealth of wisdom, its sentences are weightier with each repeated reading, and such are its values and virtues that it may be said if one properly read this Book he would not need the other nine for a possible shipwreck selection for the Bible would keep him from shipwreck! Other books are valuable: the Bible is priceless! Other books may introduce you to the silver kingdom of letters: this Book will bow you into the golden domain of revelation. Other books may bear international copyright: the Bible is copyright in heaven. "Forever, O Lord, thy word is settled in heaven" (Ps. 119:89). Other books know the stumbling frailties of time: this Book is ageless. Other books find limitation in locality with language or setting, provincial or national: this Book is universal.

Old John Gill said of the Bible, "Its depths are such that an elephant might swim, and yet in the shallows a lamb can wade."

Men of erudition have found wisdom's deepest secrets buried here, and yet the humble washerwoman has gone about her tasks and down to her lonely deathbed, quoting, "Let not your heart be troubled: ye believe in God, believe also in Me. In my Father's house are many mansions: if it were not so, I would have told you. I go to prepare a place for you. And if I go and prepare a place for you, I will come again, and receive you unto Myself; that where I am, there ye may be also" (John 14:1-3).

No course in literature is half complete without some knowledge of the Bible. What abounding praise this Book has received from the point of view of its literary excellence! But did you ever ask yourself how these sixty-six books happened to emanate on such a high level? Critics unite in pointing out the unevenness of the writings of Shelley and Keats, of Dickens and Thackeray, but such unevenness is not discovered in these Sacred Writings. Variety is there, ruggedness and softness, thunder and the still small voice, but the great contrasts only set forth the high quality of all the writings, whether produced by prophet or peasant centuries before Christ or in the first century of this era.

How amusing the errors of some respected writers! A critic well says, "If Keats had been writing a sonnet as an exercise in history, his mark would have been below passing, for he gives Cortez credit for doing what Balboa did." However, the critic is kind enough to add, "But the feeling is the same, regardless of the name, and the sonnet is nonetheless great because of its blemish." The Bible makes no such apology nor is such concession necessary. The writers of the Scripture do not say, "Let us tell lies that truth may be known," anymore than they say, "Let us do evil that good may come of it."

If you would have something of the wonder of the Bible seize you, you have only to observe its exactness and gaze upon the beautiful unity of this volume and realize it is the production of many writers separated by time and continent and most of them extremely limited in training and experience. Now, think of the possibility of selecting forty men today—not the herdsmen and fishermen of today, but comb the universities and laboratories, churches and monasteries, and when you have forty of the intellectual elite, give *them* the task of writing a Bible. If there is such a thing as moral evolution, surely these men with their advantages and in the light of general progress should do better *today* than the poor benighted writers who lived in an isolated section of this earth—a little strip approximately 150 by 50 miles and that strip not even having direct access to either of the two great oceans.

Surely our age has the necessary intellectual equipment to write a Bible. The universities have been teaching writing in every branch of its technique. Literary critics and experts abound. Surely our age has all of the mechanical equipment to produce something better than the Bible. Did Moses have a typewriter or Isaiah a dictaphone? We can't imagine the Apostle Paul pushing a button and saying, "Take a letter to the Corinthians." We have lifted our mechanics, but we lack their dynamic.

A better explanation of the composition of the Scriptures has never been given than this, in its own words: "All Scripture is given by inspiration of God" (II Tim. 3:16). "For the prophecy came not in old time by the will of man: but holy men of God spake as they were moved by the Holy Ghost" (II Pet. 1:21).

It is always surprising that there are so many people who have not discovered the glory of the Scripture. Some even say they have tried to read the Bible and have found nothing in it; which always reminds me of the saying of Goethe, "whoever reproaches an author with obscurity should first examine himself to know if all is clear within." "In the twilight," says he, "a very plain writing is illegible."

The Psalmist offers up his prayer, "Open thou mine eyes, that I may behold wondrous things out of thy law" (Ps. 119:18).

There are light readers who touch a verse here and a chapter there. There are lounging readers who start out to read with diligence but who with a yawn sprawl out over three or four sentences. There are few who read with eagerness, but it can be done. You can almost feel the thrill of the Psalmist as he said, "I rejoice at Thy word, as one that findeth great spoil" (Ps. 119:162).

However, the village of Eagerness is just three miles away, and the milestones are marked Regularity, Interest, Persistence.

The Abbe, Winkleman, classical writer on the fine arts, speaks of the perfection of the sculpture in the Appollo Belvedere, and says to the young artists, "Go and study it; and if you see no great beauty to captivate you, go again; and if you still discover none, go again and again. Go until you feel it, for be assured it is there."

So we would say of the Bible, and so the Bible itself extends invitation: "Search the Scriptures." "Study." "Meditate." "Compare Scripture with Scripture." All of these words suggest regular, persistent, attentive reading of the Word of God. And so the Apostle exhorts, "Let the word of Christ dwell in you richly," or as some translate it, "plenteously" (Col. 3:16). "Let the word of Christ dwell in you plenteously." Have good, substantial portions of His Word in your mind and in your heart, to be held there as permanent possessions.

Acquaintance with the Bible finds response among those who are broad in their interests. If a business man cannot think beyond a dollar to be made, this Book may be dull. If a farmer lives, moves, and has his being in the realm of crops, he may be bored by the Bible. But those who live beyond their occupations, those who read and imagine and dream, will find food for their dreams in its pages.

But, having said this, it needs to be said that the greatest distaste for the Bible comes from the fact of sin. The Bible is unsparing and is without compromise. Sin cannot comfortably sit in its presence. For two or three centuries men have written on the fly-leaf of presentation Bibles, "This Book will keep you from sin, or sin will keep you from this Book." My dear friend, Dr. R. A. Torrey, when approached by men who would say, "I no longer believe the Bible," would ask, "What have you been doing?" Sometimes they acknowledged he was right. Yes, the Bible carries the conviction of sin but it also carries the promise of salvation from sin through the Redeemer revealed in its pages.

And are we not here referring to the Bible's chief value? It is unique in that it is the only revelation of God in this form, and it persists because it has an ageless response to the need of every human heart. While undoubtedly of the highest literary excellence, with moral standards too high for imitation by other religious books, the Bible above and beyond these virtues is a mirror in which men see their failures and a lifeline lowered to lift them out of their defeats.

> *O may I love Thy precious Word:*
> *May I explore the mine,*
> *May I its fragrant flowers glean,*
> *May light upon me shine!*
> *O may I find my armor there:*
> *Thy Word my trusty sword,*
> *I'll learn to fight with every foe*
> *The battle of the Lord.*

CHRIST BEFORE PILATE

WHY MEN TURN BACK FROM CHRIST

Search everywhere, but you will find nobody to offer you what Christ does. He has the words of eternal life.

Consider why some turned away from Him.

There were determined doubters. They had seen the water turned to wine, the sick healed, the dead raised, the five loaves multiplied, and yet they asked, "What sign showest thou?" They were determined to doubt Him. They did not want to believe.

Some doubted to arrive at certainty. Thomas did not believe the resurrection story until he came to that great confession, "My Lord and my God!" Saul of Tarsus after his era of persecuting became a changed man, a regenerated man.

Others were disappointed. They looked for an earthly kingdom.

You can search everywhere, but you will find no one to offer you what Christ does. He has the words of eternal life.

—THE REV. PETER F. WALL,
Santa Monica, Calif.,
Assistant Director of The Bible Fellowship.

CHRIST BEFORE PILATE

By Dr. Gordon H. Clark, Ph. D.
Associate Professor of Philosophy, Wheaton College

"Then Pilate therefore took Jesus and scourged Him.
And the soldiers platted a crown of thorns and put it on
His head, and they put on Him a purple robe, and said,
Hail, King of the Jews! and they smote Him with their
hands. Pilate therefore went forth again and saith unto
them, Behold, I bring Him forth to you that ye may know
that I find no fault in Him. Then came Jesus forth, wearing
the crown of thorns and the purple robe. And Pilate saith
unto them, Behold the Man! When the chief priests therefore and officers saw Him, they cried out, saying, Crucify
Him, crucify Him. Pilate saith unto them, Take ye Him
and crucify Him; for I find no fault in Him."

Twice in this short passage, Pilate, expressing his opinion
of Jesus Christ, says, "I find no fault in Him." The second
time the conjunction of thoughts is peculiar. The text reads,
"Crucify Him, for I find no fault in Him." By all logic
Pilate ought to have said, "Release Him, for I find no fault
in Him," but with a disregard of consistency and rationality,
Pilate adjudged Christ innocent and condemned Him as
guilty. The paradox invites examination.

As the chief priests and officers brought vociferous
charges of blasphemy and sedition against Jesus, as the
soldiers scourged Him and placed the crown of thorns on
His head as they smote Him with their hands and spat in
His face, as the mob clamored for the crucifixion of the
patient Prisoner, Pilate gradually gathered that he was
judging an extraordinary person.

The Jews had already condemned Him in their own courts, and now they brought Him before the civil government for the death penalty. Nor would a humane execution satisfy them. They had seen Him scourged and yet they demanded a crueler punishment. "Crucify Him!" Fully conscious of the injustice of the charges, as clearly aware of the pains of the cross before Him as of the sting of the scourge just experienced, Jesus "is brought as a lamb to the slaughter, and as a sheep before her shearers is dumb, so He openeth not His mouth."

Pilate knew that the accusations were unjust. He knew that they had been brought only through the unreasonable jealousy of the scribes and Pharisees. Having heard of the reputation of the prisoner for going about doing good, for healing the sick, for cleansing the lepers, Pilate knew that the common people heard Jesus gladly. And by the dignified conduct of Jesus in court, Pilate knew that he was judging an extraordinary Person; but he did not know how extraordinary that Person was.

He did not know, for example, that his relation to this apparently obscure Galilean would make him more famous than all his equals—the other Roman governors, more famous than all his superiors, more famous than the Emperor himself, that in fact his name would be on the lips of countless thousands for ages to come as week after week they repeat, "born of the Virgin Mary, suffered under Pontius Pilate."

Pilate knew that this man had said something, not very serious or seditious, about being king of the Jews; but he did not know that in awful truth he was King of kings and Lord of lords. He might have guessed that this carpenter from Nazareth could make a table or a chair, but it never entered his mind that "by Him were all things created, that are in heaven, and that are in earth, visible and invisible, whether they be thrones, or dominions, or principalities, or powers; all things were created by Him, and for Him."

Pilate knew that he, the judge, had power to save Jesus from the pains of the cross; but he did not know that Jesus, the prisoner, had power to save him from the pains of hell forever. He knew, of course, and boasted of it, that he had power to release Jesus or to crucify Him; but he did not know that he had no power at all against Jesus except what was given him from above; he did not know that no man took Christ's life from Him, but that Christ could lay it down and take it again. Pilate did not know that it was this Jesus who gave him the power of which he boasted.

Pilate knew—how could he not know it—that if he let this Man go, the howling Jewish mob would break through the palace doors, trample over the soldiers, and tear Pilate limb from limb; but he did not know that he had the opportunity of being what thousands of Christians would have died thousands of deaths to be: he did not know that he had the opportunity of being the first Christian martyr.

Stephen, to whom God granted this distinction, and the apostles, who with one exception suffered violent deaths for their faith, appropriately refrained from florid reflections on martyrdom. But sub-apostolic literature reveals clearly the attitude of those faithful Christians who faced persecution to glorify God and to transmit the gospel to posterity.

About the year 108, Ignatius was arrested for being a Christian and was taken to Rome for execution. On his journey to Rome, delegates from the churches of the regions through which he passed came to pay their respects. There was a college student of the twentieth century who with the modern lack of historical perspective, was inclined to doubt the evidence, because, as he naively argued, if Ignatius had been arrested for being a Christian, his visitors also would run the risk of arrest and death. The modern student, unacquainted with true Christianity, thought no one would willingly run that risk. But that noble army— men and boys, the matron and the maid—climbed the steep ascent of heaven through peril, toil, and pain, and regarded it as an honor highly to be prized to meet the tyrant's brandished steel, the lion's gory mane. Thus, Ignatius, fearing perhaps an attempt at a rescue, wrote ahead to the Romans: "I am dying willingly for God's sake, if you do not hinder it. I beseech you, be not an unseasonable kindness to me. Suffer me to be eaten by the beasts, through whom I can attain to God. I am God's wheat, and I am ground by the teeth of wild beasts that I may be found pure bread of Christ . . . I long for the beasts that are prepared for me, and I pray that that may be found prompt for me. I will even entice them to devour me promptly. . . . Let there come on me fire and cross and struggles with wild beasts, cutting and tearing asunder. . . . Cruel tortures of the devil, may I but attain to Jesus Christ."

About fifty years later, Polycarp, the only person remaining who had seen the apostles, suffered a similar fate with similar rejoicing. When asked to say, "Lord Caesar," and save his life, he refused. Since the Christians rejected the pagan gods and were thus considered atheists, the officer asked Polycarp to say, "Away with the atheists." Hear the account of what then occurred: "Polycarp, with a stern countenance, looked on all the crowd of lawless heathen in the arena, and waving his hand at them, he groaned and looked up to heaven and said, 'Away with the atheists.' But when the pro-consul pressed him and said, 'Take the oath and I let you go; revile Christ'; Polycarp said, 'For eighty and six years have I been His servant, and He has done me no wrong; how can I blaspheme my king Who saved me?'"

And as they lit the fire, he prayed, "I bless Thee that Thou hast granted me this day and hour, that I may share, among the number of martyrs, in the cup of Thy Christ, for the resurrection to everlasting life, both of soul and body in the immortality of the Holy Spirit."

Not recognizing Jesus for what in truth He was, and blind to the opportunity of being the first Christian martyr, Pilate allowed the occasion to pass by. In his eyes, the judging of this Man was merely a part of his routine business, and he failed to grasp the significance of what was taking place.

In Philadelphia, there is an immense canvas some twenty feet wide and thirteen feet high, on which a consummate artist with vividness and skill has depicted this scene. Caiaphas, conscious of his position and power, is addressing the governor; perched on a high seat, with his back against the wall, is a scribe, haughty and contemptuous; on a bench close to the judgment seat, almost under Caiaphas' outstretched arm, there rests a portly Pharisee, wealthy and insolent; crouching in a corner, three priests heatedly discuss the case among themselves; in the mob, which is held somewhat in check by a Roman soldier, an impudent halfwit with a giggling sneer leans over to peer curiously into the face of the central figure; an enterprising gentleman in the rear tries to climb over the heads and shoulders of those in front of him to give assistance to Caiaphas in his speech of accusation; and an advocate of direct action, impatient of delay, throws up both arms, opens mouth and lungs, and yells, "Crucify Him!"

Just off center stands Jesus. His calm is a contrast for the mob's clamor. His erect dignity makes even Caiaphas appear slightly rattle-brained. But He seems unmindful of the circumstances and the proceedings as His even look moves quietly beyond the Roman tribunal to a serene contemplation of the eternal decrees of God.

And on the massive judgment seat sits the Roman Pilate, the imperial executive, the efficient governor—worried, puzzled, and burdened with indecision.

Just as some blind, inartistic souls who look upon this canvas, see the paint but not the picture, so, too, Pilate, blind to God's masterpiece, saw the prisoner but not the Person. The human artist, Munkacsy, called his painting, *Christ before Pilate,* but one may reverently imagine that God called the original scene *Pilate before Christ.* For, as Jesus stood in the presence of Pilate, Pilate sat in the presence of God.

And, though he tried, he could not escape pronouncing judgment. Once and then a second time, he protested to the Jews, "I find no fault in Him."

More recently other men as blind as Pilate, and with less excuse, have repeated Pilate's sentiment. To choose outstanding examples of a century ago, the great William E. Channing said, "I contemplate Him [Jesus] with a veneration second only to that with which I look upward to God." David Strauss confessed, "He represents within the religious sphere, the highest point beyond which humanity cannot go." And Ernest Renan admitted, "Whatever may be the surprises of the future, this Jesus will never be surpassed; none greater than He has been born among the children of men."

Is the true Christian delighted when he hears these words of praise? To be sure, these tributes from Pilate, from last century's liberals, and from this century's radicals, bear witness to an extraordinary personality. But it is to be feared that this praise of Jesus is but a device to rob Him of His transcendent glory; what they say sounds excellent, but their silence is Satanic. They find no fault in Him; neither do they find the fulness of the Godhead bodily. In effect they say, with the same disregard of logic, "Crucify Him, for I find no fault in Him."

We, too, in hearing the name of Jesus Christ, are brought face to face with God. And we, too, ought to say, "I find no fault in Him," but let us say it in a different sense and with a different connotation. Let us say it, not with a recognition of something vaguely extraordinary, but with a clear understanding of the Person. Consider His active obedience and perfect righteousness. Reflect on His purpose to redeem His own by a propitiatory sacrifice to God the Father. Contemplate the mystery of a divine and a human nature united inconfusedly and inseparably in one divine Person. Believe on Him; trust in Him; accept Him as Lord and worship the adorable Person of the God-Man.

> *My Lord, my Master, at Thy feet adoring,*
> *I see Thee bowed beneath Thy load of woe:*
> *For me, a sinner, is Thy life-blood pouring;*
> *For Thee, my Savior, scarce my tears will flow.*
>
> *My Lord, My Savior, when I see Thee wearing*
> *Upon Thy bleeding brow the crown of thorn,*
> *Shall I for pleasure live, or shrink from bearing*
> *Whate'er my lot may be of pain or scorn?*
>
> *O Victim of Thy Love! O pangs most healing!*
> *O saving death! O wounds that I adore!*
> *O shame most glorious! Christ, before Thee kneeling,*
> *I pray Thee keep me Thine forevermore.*

THE UNIVERSAL SINFULNESS
OF MAN

THE GREAT PHYSICIAN'S DIAGNOSIS

"When we were yet without strength, in due time Christ died for the ungodly" (Rom. 5:6). That means He died for those who were lost.

We are members of a rebellious race. For myself, when I read the third chapter of Romans or the first chapter of Genesis, I have no complaint. I am correctly described; my picture is there in the book.

I am glad that Christ as the Great Physician does not try to fool the patient with a false diagnosis. If God's Word tells us that we are members of a corrupt and a guilty race, we ought at once to take the remedy.

It is a wonderful thing that we members of the race of Adam can be saved. I hope the newness of it will never wear off. I cannot lose the sense of astonishment that Christ died for me when I was His enemy.

Dr. J. Oliver Buswell, Jr.,
Former President, Wheaton College.

THE UNIVERSAL SINFULNESS OF MAN

By Dr. Isaac Page, D. D.
District Secretary, China Inland Mission;
Speaker at Fall Evangelistic Services

I COMMEND to you, students, a book by Horatius Bonar entitled *God's Way of Holiness*. In this book, he takes up the question of the believer and the law, a subject that needs to be made clear to many in these days of loose thinking.

Let us turn to Rom. 3:9: "They are all under sin." Whether we be Jew or Gentile, we are under sin and consequently under the curse. The sword of Damocles is hanging over our heads, waiting to fall. No member of the race has ever fulfilled the demands of a righteous God expressed in His law, for "there is none righteous, no, not one."

But, you say, "I am pretty good." Well, did you ever covet anything? Then you have broken God's law. The straight-edge of God's law shows that we are out of line, and the verdict is, "There is none righteous, there is none that seeketh after God." We hear men talking ponderously about *seeking* after truth, when Jesus tells us, "I am the way, the truth, and the life."

Of Jew and Gentile alike, the Scripture declares, "There is none that doeth good, no, not one. Their throat is an open sepulcher." Just visit a graveyard where erosion or storm has opened a grave and understand how repulsive is this picture of sin. It nauseates and defiles. One day when Mrs. Page and I were traveling in China, we came across a grave from which the rains had washed the soil. It was a distressing and noisome sight. Such is the repulsiveness of our sin in the sight of a holy God, who says of sinners, "Their throat is an open sepulcher."

How can a Christian keep his radio turned on all day Sunday for the programs of the world and keep in fellowship with God? The jazz programs of our day allow no rest. There is no rest in jazz. The works of the devil make men restless. There is rest in Christ, but never in the world.

There are at least fourteen different words for sin in the New Testament, bearing evidence of the universal reign of sin. Wherever one turns in the Bible, he finds a picture of man fallen into sin and in need of a Savior.

A middle-aged woman who had just come over from the old country and seemed eager to learn the English language received a dictionary as a gift from her neighbor. She spent time with it each evening. A short time later, when the friend asked her how she liked the volume, she answered, "It's a wonderful book, but it do change the subject so often."

"It do change the subject so often!" Not so with the Bible, however, for the Scripture tells over and over the story of man in sin and his need of the Savior.

There is a day coming when you and I are going to stand beside the crystal sea. Are you going to stand justified before God? Every sin will be reviewed. Can it be possible that you will appear stainless, that you will be without any blemish?

Every word that you have ever spoken is recorded. First of all, it is recorded in the tablets of your memory. Then it is recorded also in God's book. In that day when men shall stand before God, every mouth shall be stopped—there can be no excuses. Every man shall stand condemned or not condemned by his acts and his words. Never believe that you can get away from your sin. You may as well try to get away from your shadow. This problem can only be solved by the acceptance of Jesus Christ, Who shed His precious blood to redeem us from our sin. We must accept Him as Savior and Lord.

"According to Thy law, O Lord, I know I am a sinner. I want Jesus Christ to become my Savior." Can you say this, dear friend? If you have never taken the Lord before, will you not take Him this morning? Some of you young men have been playing with sin. This morning, will you say, "I need such a Savior"! If you are willing, why not take Him now?

> *Into my heart, into my heart;*
> *Come into my heart, Lord Jesus.*
> *Come in today, come in to stay;*
> *Come into my heart, Lord Jesus.*

THE UNANSWERABLE QUESTION

MAKING GLAD MEN OF SAD MEN

Cares of this life press home to us the three aspects of our salvation: the foundation of salvation, the assurance of salvation, the joy of salvation.

The foundation of salvation is a fact. It remains a fact whether you believe it or not. The fact is, He loved me and gave Himself for me. Christ died for me.

The assurance of salvation is also a reality. At one time in his youth, Dr. James M. Gray had no assurance. When he read John 5:24, he rushed suddenly into a friend's room and shouted, "I have assurance."

The joy of salvation comes by a simple formula. The word *joy* is a simple word. J stands for Jesus; Y stands for you; O stands between them and stands for nothing, too. Let nothing come, whatever you do, between the Lord Jesus and you.

D. H. DOLMAN,
Elmswell Rectory, Bury St. Edmunds, Eng.,
Former Christian worker among the Jews of Germany.

THE UNANSWERABLE QUESTION

By Dr. Henry C. Thiessen, D. D., Ph. D.
Chairman, Department of Bible, Theology, and Philosophy,
Wheaton College

There are many unanswerable questions in life. Many others we can answer only in part. We cannot say how a holy being could fall; we cannot fathom the mystery of the Trinity; we cannot tell why so much graft, murder, and licentiousness remain unpunished in this life. Neither can we say why God permitted sin to enter this fair universe, except in the general way incidental in His self-revelation.

Fortunately, we do not need to know the answers to these questions; for no serious consequences arise from our inability to answer them. But there is one question that is supremely *the* unanswerable question, and it is one that we must nevertheless consider. It is stated in Heb. 2:3: "How shall we escape, if we neglect so great salvation; which at the first began to be spoken by the Lord, and was confirmed unto us by them that heard Him."

Let us consider the implications of this question. We notice:

I. *The Greatness of This Salvation.* The writer speaks of it as *"so great a salvation."* What is it that makes this salvation great?

There is, first, the greatness of its Author. The salvation through faith in Jesus Christ is not the invention of some metaphysician or cloistered monk but of God Himself. He Who is infinite in wisdom, love, and power planned, provided, and proclaims it. Therefore, those who reject this

35

salvation reject the plan and provision of the Creator, Preserver, and Governor of the universe. Soon after Calvin Coolidge returned to private life, a New York newspaper engaged him to contribute a daily article of from one hundred and fifty to two hundred words. They promised to pay him two dollars a word for each article. What made his contributions so valuable? Why, the position he had occupied! He was considered to have wide knowledge and experience and would therefore know the solution to our national problems. Many of us would have had to pay the same paper to have our contributions accepted, unless they should appear in an inconspicuous "Opine" column, but Mr. Coolidge was well paid for his contributions. So this salvation is the thought and work of God, and to neglect it is to insult an infinite intelligence, will, and love.

Again, it is great because of its cost. It is commonly agreed that that which does not cost much isn't worth much, and in general this is true. But it is not true that the thing must cost *us* much to be worth much: it may be that someone else has borne the expense and that we may have it without cost because another has paid the price of it. This salvation cost God the best that He had. It cost Him His only Son. All the universe could not compare in value to His only begotten Son. This salvation is so great because of its infinite cost.

Then it is great also because of its intrinsic worth. The cost of a thing does not always indicate its true value. An unfortunate explorer may be cast upon a lonely island with diamonds in his possession but of what value are these against a persistent and painful hunger? How much more valuable is bread and other wholesome food than the things whose value is only extrinsic? The salvation of Christ is not intended for ornamentation; it is not an article for the mantle-piece but food for the heart. It has the power to save a man from the lowest hell to the highest heaven. It can take the hardened sinner, the vile and depraved, the self-righteous and the debauched, and make him into a child of God. It is able to save and keep saved. This salvation is so great because of what it can do if it gets a real chance at the human heart.

And then it is also great because of its availability. Some of the greatest things in life are accessible to all, such as air and water. Suppose there were a sure cure for tuberculosis and leprosy but the price was prohibitive for the poor and the quantity limited. Would not all the poor sufferers of these dreaded diseases strive for money with which to purchase the remedy and would they not hurry before the supply gave out? But this salvation is great because it is free; it may be had without money and without price. And the supply is inexhaustible. Speaking of the value of the death of Christ, Hodge says: "Nothing different and nothing more would have been required had every child of Adam been saved through His blood." We preach the inexhaustible riches of Christ. This salvation is so great because it is available to all.

II. *The Danger of Failing to Obtain this Salvation.* Although the salvation of Christ is so great, multitudes never experience the values of it. It is a sign of the blindness of the human heart and of the sluggishness of the human will. Men fail of the benefits of salvation not primarily because of what they are, such as murderers, liars, adulterers, but because of what they fail to do. "Though Christ a thousand times in Bethlehem be born; if He's not born in thee, thy soul is still forlorn." The remedy has been provided. The fountain for sin and uncleanness has been opened, but the spiritual leper must plunge therein. Salvation is unrealized because it remains unappropriated. People are lost through simple neglect of the salvation God has provided. Various things cause people to neglect this salvation.

Preoccupation keeps many from accepting Christ. How many people are so busy with secondary things that they have no time to pay attention to that which is primary! "The cares of this world, and the deceitfulness of riches, and the lusts of other things entering in, choke the Word, and it becometh unfruitful" (Mark 4:19). The Holy Spirit seeks to get the attention of people: "Behold, *behold,* BEHOLD, I stand at the door and knock: if any man hear My voice, and open the door, I will come in to him, and will sup with him, and he with Me" (Rev. 3:20). If it isn't one's daily toil and care, then it is the movie or the newspaper or the radio or the gambling den or some other den of vice. Like the eagle on a cake of ice on a frosty and misty morning, who was devouring a carrion as he glided slowly toward the precipice of Niagara! With one shriek he went down to destruction when he found that he was frozen fast to the cake on which he had sat and enjoyed himself. So many are too much occupied with their own affairs to give the interests of their soul any attention.

Skepticism is a barrier to others. Many are kept away from Christ because of so-called "mental difficulties" with the Bible. Satan has whispered to them the old doubt of Eden: "Yea, hath God said" (Gen. 3:1). They are "troubled" about the miracles, the virgin birth, the atonement, the verbal inspiration of the Bible. They have heard some noted "scholar" deny all these doctrines, and they have come to believe that it is scholarly to repeat this silly prattle. But however unsettled any man on earth may be as to these eternal facts, the Psalmist gave expression to an abiding fact when he exclaimed: "Forever, O Lord, Thy Word is settled in heaven" (Ps. 119:89). Are you neglecting your salvation because of the babblings of unbelievers? Remember that in some cases it is not primarily a mental difficulty but a moral one that keeps men away from God.

Procrastination keeps others from Christ. Many neglect salvation on the ground that they will attend to it at some more convenient day. Yet all the day long God has stretched out His hands of invitation to them, and all the day long they have remained indifferent to God's offer of grace. They have hardened their necks and so find it easy to remain indifferent. They have blinded their eyes and stopped their ears lest they should feel convicted of their sin. Is it any wonder that God says to such as these: "Because I have called, and ye refused; I have stretched out My hand, and no man regarded; but ye have set at nought all my counsel, and would none of my reproof: I also will laugh at your calamity; I will mock when your fear cometh. . . . Then shall they call upon Me, but I will not answer; they will seek Me diligently, but they shall not find Me" (Prov. 1:24-28). Therefore, "Today if ye will hear His voice, harden not your hearts, as in the provocation" (Heb. 3:15). "Behold, now is the accepted time; behold, now is the day of salvation" (II Cor. 6:2).

III. *The Impossibility of Escaping After Neglecting This Salvation.* The answer to this *unanswerable* question is this: that those who neglect this salvation shall not escape. This may be proved in a logical way.

There is, first, the fact that all must appear before the judgment seat of God. "It is appointed unto men once to die, and after this the judgment" (Heb. 9:27). God "hath appointed a day, in the which He will judge the world in righteousness by that man whom He hath ordained; whereof He hath given assurance unto all men, in that He hath raised Him from the dead" (Acts 17:31). The resurrection of Christ is not only a proof of the fact that Jesus is the Son of God (Rom. 1:4) but also the assurance that all men must appear before Him for judgment. The Scriptures declare that all shall be assembled before Him, the small and the great, that death, the sea, and hades shall give up the dead in them, so that they may stand before the Great White Throne for judgment. There is no possibility of escaping this gathering before the judgment throne of God.

Then also, God knows your record. When Jesus was on earth He "needed not that any should testify of man: for He knew what was in man" (John 2:25). The writer to the Hebrews says: "Neither is there any creature that is not manifest in His sight: but all things are naked and opened unto the eyes of Him with whom we have to do" (Heb. 4:13). God, therefore, is in a position to judge righteously, seeing He knows all about every man. Human courts may return a false verdict; human witnesses may be mistaken or may perjure themselves; but God knows all the facts and circumstances. There is no appeal from His decision, for He judges in the light of absolute fact.

And, further, God has warned man of the consequences of disobedience and unbelief. "He that believeth on the Son hath everlasting life: and he that believeth not the Son shall not see life; but the wrath of God abideth on him" (John 3:36). God told Adam and Eve what would happen if they ate of the forbidden tree (Gen. 2:16-17), and He tells us, "The soul that sinneth, it shall die" (Ezek. 18:4, 20). "Know ye not that the unrighteous shall not inherit the kingdom of God?" (I Cor. 6:9). The context in Hebrews 2 tells us that the word spoken by angels was stedfast and every transgression and disobedience of the Law, given by angelic ministration, received a just recompense; and it asks us how we may hope to escape, seeing the gospel message began to be spoken by the Lord Himself. Ignorance of the law excuses no one, although it may affect the degree of the penalty; but who is there in America who can plead ignorance of the Word and will of God?

Finally, God will not accept substitutes. Jesus declared: "Many will say to me in that day, Lord, Lord, have we not prophesied in Thy name? and in Thy name have cast out devils? and in Thy name done wonderful works? And then will I profess unto them, I never knew you: depart from Me, ye that work iniquity" (Matt. 7:22-23). Good works, outward morality, even church membership and church work cannot take the place of a personal experience of grace in the heart. D. L. Moody once said that some people are like the foolish farmer who painted his pump because the water was dirty and unfit to drink. What good does it do to clean up the outside if the trouble is on the inside? Jesus spoke of some men as "whited sepulchers" full of dead men's bones. He also said to make the tree good, and its fruit will be good; for "a good tree cannot bring forth evil fruit, neither can a corrupt tree bring forth good fruit" (Matt. 7:18). "He that hath the Son hath life; and he that hath not the Son of God hath not the life" (I John 5:12). "There is none other name under heaven given among men, whereby we must be saved" (Acts 4:12).

From all these things, we see how impossible it is to escape the judgment of God if we continue to neglect so great a salvation. Will you not, dear friend, this moment give more earnest heed to the things you have heard, lest by any means you let them slip? Will you listen to that knock at your heart's door right now and let the Savior come in? If so, then you will not need to be anxious about the future but will be able to face it with confidence and deep joy. God grant that you may not be lost for simply neglecting this great salvation!

FOOTPRINTS OF AN
OLD TESTAMENT MAN

ASSURANCE IN A MOMENT OF DOUBT

As the days in Herod's prison go on, John the Baptist finds himself facing ignominious death. There comes to his mind this question: "Art thou He that should come or do we look for another?" Our Lord sends back these equally enigmatic words, "Blessed is he whosoever shall not be offended in Me."

What can we learn from this question and answer? You may be called to a place of service where the manifest blessing of God will be upon your life. John had his apprenticeship out in the wilderness eating locusts and wild honey, and then in the providence of God he came preaching repentance. How John rejoiced in that period of ministry when he was a bright and shining light! But that was not all of God's plan for John, for as though by eclipse, he found himself in the dark-shadowed gloom of Herod's prison. It took him time to adjust his spiritual vision to the darkness. I doubt that he was completely adjusted when he sent his disciples to Jesus.

When we are suddenly silenced, dropped from a high place, we begin to wonder, was the vision we had true? I suggest to your hearts if that comes to be your condition in life, get some of the sweetness of this promise. However unanswerable may be the doubt, remember, "Blessed is he that is not offended in Me."

DR. V. RAYMOND EDMAN,
Acting President, Wheaton College.

FOOTPRINTS OF AN OLD TESTAMENT MAN

By Dr. Walter L. Wilson, M. D.
Author, *The Romance of a Doctor's Visits, etc.*

This story concerns a gentleman named Asher. His way of life has some lessons for us.

Some day your name, too, will be the subject of discussion. All that you are—your affections, your attitudes, your actions—will be brought to light, as are this gentleman's.

Jacob pronounced a blessing on Asher. His name means "happy." The Lord puts a premium on happiness. "That My joy might remain in you, and that your joy might be full" (John 15:11), reads the Scripture; and again, "The God of hope fill you with all joy" (Rom. 15:13).

Jacob blessed this son of his, Asher, and said, "Out of Asher his bread shall be fat, and he shall yield royal dainties" (Gen. 49:20). But this rascal son had fooled his old father. Asher brought in the blood-stained coat of his brother Joseph and said, "Look, father, Joseph has been killed by wild beasts." And the father wept.

Then the father learned that the brothers had sold Joseph into slavery for what would be fifty-five cents. But Jacob reminded Asher of none of these. And Moses said, "Let Asher be blessed with children." And Moses said also, "Let him dip his foot in oil" so that wherever he went he would leave behind him a footprint of beauty.

There is something of spiritual value in this incident for us, for we all leave behind us a footprint of some sort. Is it beautiful or ugly? Is it a footprint of evil we leave?

May our footprints be found in the way of the Almighty. The Lord does not always level the mountains of life into plains, but He makes us strong for climbing. He strengthens us so we shall enjoy the mountains. "Thy shoes shall be iron and brass." Such was His promise to Asher. Feet in shoes of brass walk over stones and thorns and do not feel them. Remember Habakkuk's remark, "My feet are as hind's feet." They were feet fit for the rock places.

Likewise the Lord says, "As thy days so shall thy strength be." Most of us would prefer strength to meet trouble before the trouble comes, but God does not promise that. It is as the difficulty arises, as the blow comes, that the Lord in His grace gives the ability to meet it.

If the spirituality we possess doesn't suit us, it will not be attractive to anybody else. If we go out to tell the story of divine love and grace, our lives must exhibit fruit-bearing and happiness. We must be prepared for people who look at us to behold a living example.

Now, what made Asher the kind of a person who interests us? One fact: Asher had come to his brother Joseph and bowed five times before him and had been forgiven. That is why Moses doesn't mention the whole catalog of Asher's sins. Why should he? God had forgiven Asher; Jacob had forgiven. And Moses' words are the equivalent of an assertion that we need more men like Asher.

Asher gave forth "royal dainties." What do you give forth? What you give forth is probably determined by what you take in. Gossip is not the gospel, young people. Don't take it in, and you won't give it forth. My father-in-law once said to me, "You know, Walter, I think some people should have signs over their ears, 'Dirt May Be Dumped Here.'" Does that kind of thing find a place in your hearing? If you were offered a bowl of sawdust with cream and sugar you would refuse it, not because it was harmful in itself, but because it was not helpful to you. Gossip and rumor are far less helpful than a sawdust diet.

Let us learn from Asher, too, that we are to walk with feet dipped in oil, which is a type of the spiritual life. We are to leave behind us a footprint that tells the story of a walk with the Lord, a fragrant, sweet walk with God. He has promised to equip us with strength and power to walk in the spiritual way. "As thy days, so thy strength." We all should be shockproof Christians. No matter what comes, we can be able to face it sweetly, quietly, confidently, trusting in our Lord, Who said, "As thy days, so shall thy strength be."

This was the promise to Asher, and this is the promise to us. We look to the blessed Spirit of love to make the Word a blessing to every heart. We pray that the Lord will be more precious to each of us, that in the crises of life our absolute dependence for strength will be on Him.

THE INTRINSIC VALUE OF JONAH

THE CLAMOR OF FALSE PROPHETS

If we could have an hour of honest submission to God and humility before Him, the course of history might be changed, but there is little light along the lines which are at present being pursued. God is trying to teach the nations of the world that if they sin, they must pay. If they go to Tarshish when He sends them to Nineveh, they will have to settle for the fare.

If only God would give us a Jonah, whose voice could be heard, someone to walk up and down the bloody streets of the nations, to cry out to them about their sins, it seems that there might be hope, but just at present the prophets who clamor seem to be the false prophets who encourage men to sin and prophesy "Peace" to those who are in rebellion against God.

THE LATE DR. CHARLES A. BLANCHARD,
Former President of Wheaton College.

THE INTRINSIC VALUE OF JONAH

By Dr. Jacob J. Hoffmann, Ph. D.
Associate Professor of Theology, Wheaton College

> *Now the word of the Lord came unto Jonah the son of Amittai, saying, Arise, go to Nineveh, that great city, and cry against it; for their wickedness is come up before me.* — Jonah 1:1-2

I HAVE no apology to make if I appear on this platform with a message on the prophet Jonah.

Wheaton College stands for everything that is "for Christ and His kingdom." In the experience and destiny of Jonah, nothing less is involved than "Christ and His kingdom."

Except perhaps the Pentateuch and Isaiah, no book of the Bible has suffered so severely at the hands of the critics as has the Book of Jonah. There are two main reasons for this: first, scholars have overlooked or ignored the historical background of the first period of Jonah's prophetic ministry; second, they fail to see, or they ignore the psychological element in the prophet's religious convictions.

I. THE HISTORICAL BACKGROUND OF THE FIRST PERIOD OF JONAH'S PROPHETIC ACTIVITY

Whenever the kingdom of God in Israel faced a crisis, invariably a prophet appeared upon the scene of conflicting interests. As Ezekiel, for example, he could spy out impending danger from his lofty prophetic watch-tower. "Son of man, I have made thee a watchman unto the house of Israel: therefore hear the word at My mouth, and give them warning from me" (3:17).

The greatest crisis in the theocratic history up to the inception of the tenth century was the separation of the king-

51

dom under the autocratic, despotic son of Solomon. Mono-theism, faith in the one true God and the unity of religion and worship, was at stake.

Jeroboam I, heading the list of northern kingdom rulers, was a shrewd politician and diplomat. Knowing religion to be the strongest cementing power in national life, he created religious shrines at the southern and northern boundaries of the kingdom, thereby menacing kingdom solidarity that came from unified worship at Jerusalem. This besetting national sin of idolatry introduced by Jero-boam finally wrecked both the southern and northern king-doms of Israel.

In vain Abijah raised a protesting voice of warning; in vain Elijah stemmed himself against the down-grade life. On Mt. Carmel, the Tishbite had once more saved the day but only for another night that was to spell disaster for the northern kingdom.

In the last half of the ninth century B.C., Jeroboam II became king of the northern kingdom. Jonah's activity as counselor and aid to Jeroboam in promoting the interests of the northern kingdom and in saving it for the theocracy came during the first half of this powerful ruler's reign. In the earlier, better days of Jeroboam, Jonah had predicted Jehovah's returning the territory Israel had lost to its ene-mies during an hour of humiliation and weakness. Jeroboam accordingly restored the coasts of Israel from Hamath down past the Dead Sea to Elath, northeastern wing of the Red Sea. Prosperity was detrimental to Jeroboam, how-ever, for he ascribed his success to personal wisdom and power rather than to God's goodness. He fell back into the sins of his predecessor, and Jonah's faithful ministry utterly failed of its purpose.

II. THE SECOND CALL OF JONAH

In the midst of these fruitless activities came Jonah's call to Nineveh. This charge meant supporting the deadliest enemy of his own people and of the kingdom of God. Jonah was in a position we can hardly appreciate. A terrific inner conflict with conscience, convictions, and divine mission tormented him. Did Jehovah change His purpose? Had He become unfaithful to His covenant with Israel? Was He inconsistent with His own character? Up to now, Jonah's life had been his unwavering faith in Jehovah; and the power of his life, Jehovah's unfailing promise of Israel's redemption. Now this anchorage seemed to slip away. Jonah became confused; he could not find his way out of the dilemma and despaired of life. Instead of going eastward toward Nineveh, he turned westward toward the Mediterranean Sea and embarked upon a merchantman for Spain. But where would the fugitive go? "Whither shall I go from Thy Spirit . . . flee from Thy presence?"

Being out of harmony with God's will and plan for his life, Jonah would inevitably meet trouble. By denying the right to life to 120,000 benighted souls, he forfeited the right to life himself and was consigned to his watery grave. When in the anguish of his soul Jonah cried out to God, repented, confessed, and believed, God pardoned him, however, and saved him from the jaws of death. (Not even the stomach of a sea-monster could stand a backslidden prophet!)

God insisted, nevertheless, that Jonah go to Nineveh. The possible consequences of Nineveh's repentance tortured Jonah, but he had learned to obey God. Preaching brought a whole city to sackcloth and ashes. What a contrast with Samaria and Jerusalem! This success placed Jonah in expressly the disheartening situation he wanted to prevent by his flight. (Read chapter 4:1-3.) As discouraged Elijah, tired of life, sat under the juniper tree and prayed, "Take my life!" as Paul rather wished perdition for himself if Israel could not be saved; so Jonah, rather than to see Israel destroyed, prayed: "It is better for me to die than to live!"

III. THE SYMBOLICAL MEANING OF JONAH'S CHARACTER AND LIFE

1. Jonah is a type of Christ:

a) In his humiliation and death. The Israel of Christ's time, unfaithful to God's covenant, and desirous of proof of Christ's Messiahship despite His many miracles among them, is given the sign not of Christ's glorification but of His humiliation and death on the cross.

b) In his resurrection. As the sea-monster could not keep Jonah, so the grave could not keep the Holy One of God. Christ arose "the Prince of the Kings of this world."

2. Jonah is a type of Israel.

a) Knowing the one true God, Jonah refused to make His redemptive will known to the ignorant Gentile city. By denying the right to life to the Gentiles, he forfeited the right to life himself and was punished. After due repentance, Jonah was delivered by the miraculous intervention of God.

b) Just so the Israel of Christ's day was unfaithful to God's covenant and suffered resultant trouble. Jerusalem was destroyed; the temple was burned; religious institutions of Judaism were dissolved; and Jewish exiles were sold as slaves. Israel was scattered to the four winds.

Nor are her troubles at an end now. They will increase until in the tribulation night Israel will repent, cry mightily to God, and be delivered by the miraculous personal intervention of Jehovah—Jesus.

3. Jonah is a type of the universal character of revealed religion.

Painful as the experience will continue to be, Israel's prophetism will be called upon to enter upon the divine plan of Israel's temporary rejector and to put itself at God's disposal for its execution. This is the profound mystery in the divine counsels: in the light of its New Testament setting, the rejection of Israel is to make possible "the receiving of the Gentiles." And God's free grace to the Gentiles is to justify the receiving and final restoration of Israel.

This divine symbolism of Jonah and his beloved people is perfectly illustrated and epitomized in the life and experience of St. Paul. Like Jonah, the Apostle had to feel the sorrow and agony of death by leaving his beloved people and going to the Gentiles. In his letter to the Romans, he interprets the Old Testament prophets to this effect: Salvation could come to the Gentiles only on condition of Israel's rejection. (Read Rom. 11:25.)

All of this profound and wonderfully rich symbolism in which the destiny of Israel and the nations is decided lies hidden and yet revealed in the experience and destiny of Jonah.

THE LORDSHIP OF JESUS CHRIST

CHRISTIAN STABILITY

Paul and Silas were in prison, their feet in stocks. Yet the prisoners heard their faithful testimony of song and prayer. When the earthquake freed them, the keeper cried out, "Sirs, what must I do to be saved?"

I think he meant saved, not just from the wrath of his superior officer, but in the Christian sense. He had heard Paul and Silas sing and wanted what they had. They did not say, "Go to Wheaton College and stay in that atmosphere." They said, "Believe on the Lord Jesus Christ and thou shalt be saved and thy house."

You will probably not be cast into prison and beaten, though we don't know what will happen in this world. Nevertheless, Satan will come to you and will try to lead you astray. Temptation comes to all. Your college program will not be easy; there will be academic, financial, and social problems. But flee to the Lord for refuge. Remember the stability of Christian faith. Paul and Silas remembered that in their hour of difficulty. Don't look for stability in Christian fellowship, great as that is. Stability is in God's Word.

Dr. J. Oliver Buswell, Jr.,
Former President, Wheaton College.

THE LORDSHIP OF JESUS CHRIST

By Dr. Rowland V. Bingham, D.D.
Sudan Interior Mission

In a little rural church last Sunday, I found in the morning lesson the words of Jesus, "Follow me; and let the dead bury their dead" (Matt. 8:22).

These are strong words, yet they give Christ's own demands on us. See the position He took of absolute lordship. For either He is Lord of all or He is not Lord at all.

We need to be certain of our relationship to Him. One morning I spoke in a church attended by parents of one of our missionaries. The mother had gone so far as to write her son, "You do not love me if you insist on going to Africa." He wrote back, "I love you, but I love Jesus more." Natural affection cannot come before Christ.

The Lord points to whitened harvest fields. His command still stands. You cannot wipe it out, whatever your doctrinal interpretation.

We need to face our relationship to His command. The oldest missionary we have in the Sudan came to see me thirty-seven years ago about his call to the central Sudan. He was carrying on a business while completing a medical course, was making money and owned much property. He said, "If you don't think I am the man to go, then sell all my property and send someone else in my place." After some months the little doctor wrote that he had sold his business and was studying for three months in Liverpool, England, taking post-graduate work in tropical medicine. So our committee in that city, Liverpool, investigated him. They found he was living in a squalid tenement lodging house and this raised a mental question with them, but they did not know that he was preaching and praying there every morning. At the end of three months, he wrote again to ask about the board's decision. He said he was sailing for West Africa in a week and he desired us to write to the field stating whether he had been accepted.

Was that going out on faith, in obedience to the Lord's command? What we would have done without that little man, Dr. A. P. Stirrett, in that needy field I do not know. He would run from Dan to Beersheba, as it were, for any missionary that needed him. For more than a quarter of a century he was the only doctor we had. Talk about the beloved Physician? What would Luke say? He is out there today at the age of seventy-four, giving out the gospel to all who need it.

I present to you today a work that demands more of that kind of obedience. Perhaps God has not called all of you to Africa. But each *one* of you must face the decision as to whether or not Christ is to be first in his life. You must face the question of His Lordship. If He is to be first, you will follow Him anywhere, not going back, not even looking back, but being faithful even unto the end, that you may hear Him say, "Well done, good and faithful servant."

WHAT GOD CANNOT DO

A WAY AND THE WAY

The Greek *logos* finds an interesting parallel in the Chinese word *tao*. It means way, teaching, doctrine. It is used in John 1:1, "In the beginning was the *tao* and the *tao* was with God and the *tao* was God."

It is a common word in the parlance of a philosophical people and with the word *li* (a course of reasoning, a form) it is used to designate almost any school of ethics or philosophy. The *tao* is used in John 14:6 as setting forth the Lord Jesus as THE WAY.

Dr. Lin Yutang, the author, published an article in the Forum Magazine entitled, "Why I Am a Pagan." I went with a friend to visit him in his New York apartment. When we told him that we wished to speak of the contents of his article, he asked if we agreed with his sentiments. My companion replied courteously but emphatically, "Well, *not exactly!*" He demonstrated with great ability where Dr. Lin had missed the way, for Dr. Lin asserted that the Christian concept of the *tao* is identical with the Taoist. Presently I took up the conversation, switching suddenly to the Mandarin of Peking which I knew would be readily understood, and showed that the Taoist concept of the *tao* is an ethic while the Christian revelation declares Him to be a Person.

China bleeds today. She has survived many waves of disaster. Her longevity has been due to adherence to the great primal law of filial piety, the first commandment with promise. Earthly perpetuity, however, is not eternal life. The latter can only be obtained through the Gospel of the completed work of the Son of God. It is this knowledge and faith that China and all the world so sorely needs.

Dr. James R. Graham,
Special Lecturer in Bible, Wheaton College.

WHAT GOD CANNOT DO

By Dr. John F. Walvoord, Th. D.
*Associate Professor of Systematic Theology,
Dallas Theological Seminary*

I want to consider with you this morning an aspect of the doctrine of omnipotence which is frequently overlooked, that is, what God cannot do.

We are often reminded of His great power: "Wherefore He is able also to save them to the uttermost that come unto God by Him, seeing He ever liveth to make intercession for them" (Heb. 7:25). And again, "God is able to make all grace abound toward you; that ye, always having all sufficiency in all things, may abound to every good work" (II Cor. 9:8).

It is a wonderful truth that whatever our problem, God is able; whatever our temptation, there is a way of escape for God's own. Yet there is a realm in which God cannot operate. While God is sovereign, He has outlined a domain of human responsibility; for the sovereignty of God has never destroyed the responsibility of man.

God cannot lie. The devil is a liar from the beginning. The human heart is deceitful and wicked above all things. Our only hope is that eternal life which God, Who cannot lie, has promised from the beginning. It is therefore less important to find out what man thinks than to know what God says. No matter what the field, we can believe that our God does not and cannot lie. We can come with implicit confidence to His Word. In studying it, we come to a place where we do not rest upon the frail things of human history, but find satisfaction in an inspired record.

God cannot save a soul apart from the death of Christ. This cuts through many theories of theology, but this is at the heart of Christianity. Without it, there would be no Christianity at all. "Without shedding of blood is no remission" (Heb. 9:22). "And as it is appointed unto men once to die, but after this the judgment: so Christ was once offered to bear the sins of many" (Heb. 9:27-28a). Romans three outlines the great work of God in salvation and the absolute necessity of Christ's death, not only to save you, but to save all. God is limited to the death of Christ to save souls. All the wisdom of God, all the love of God, cannot depart from this program of God, that only through the death of Christ can God save souls. How this glorifies a holy God! It makes God righteous and just when He forgives a sinner because Christ has paid the price.

The more we study it, the more we glory in it. All Christ's love and agony would not have availed for you. It was His death, His shed blood, that availed; He died for us on the cross and that agony of death has accomplished our salvation. The human torture was not the real sacrifice. The real sacrifice was in the spiritual realm. The immaculately holy One, Who had never tasted of sin, Who knew no sin, was made to be sin for us.

Can we contemplate how such a holy Person would shrink from having the whole sin of the race placed on Him? Can we think of the agony of the Christ bearing on the cross the weight of your sin and mine? We cannot comprehend all this, but we thank God that through the death of His Son we are saved. If you do not know Christ, will you turn to Him that you may have His glorious salvation?

Another *cannot* is set forth in the Scripture, this time in the field of human responsibility. *God cannot save an un-*

believer. God cannot save a soul that will not put faith in Christ. The element of human will and of human responsibility is present in the supernatural act of belief. If you sit here this morning in unbelief, that act of unbelief is damming all the grace of God as long as unbelief stands in the way.

We are taught the infinite love of God for the lost. If we could enter into a small part of this great love, if we could only realize that God is still waiting for those who are still outside the fold to come to Him—how transformed we would be! Yet we would need to look upon the lost, realizing that without faith men cannot please God. There is only one door to salvation. It has "whosoever" written on it, but all who come must enter that door. "He that believeth on Him is not condemned: but he that believeth not is condemned already, because he hath not believed in the name of the only begotten Son of God" (John 3:18).

Are you saved? If so, it is by faith. If not, it is by unbelief.

There is yet more God cannot do that He would delight to do if He could, but He has left this matter also in the realm of human responsibility. *God cannot abundantly bless an unyielded life.* Many of us can look back to a time when we were not yielded and marvel at the grace of God to us even then. But as we followed on, we may have missed a wonderful blessing. Study the Parable of the Vine and the Branches in John 15. Notice in verse ten, "If ye keep My commandments, ye shall abide in My love; even as I have kept my Father's commandments, and abide in His love."

Our disobedience does not destroy His love but it does prevent blessing in our lives. Only God knows what He could bring into your life if you were fully yielded to Him.

God has made it plain that heavenly blessings can be received now if we but put ourselves into the place of blessing. "If ye abide in Me, and my words abide in you, ye shall ask what ye will, and it shall be done unto you" (John 15:7).

Perhaps because your life has not been fully yielded to Him you have missed the best. Whatever is God's will for you, it is the best, for God has promised to bless the life that is yielded to Him.

As we study God's Word, we see not only the things God can do but the things He has left in your hands, the things God cannot do. He cannot lie. He cannot save a soul apart from the death of Christ. God cannot save an unbeliever. And, finally, God cannot abundantly bless a life not wholly yielded to Him.

STANDING FOR CHRIST
IN BUSINESS

TRIALS AND REWARDS OF TRANSLATING

Guatemala is a little country, with its 2,225,000 population divided into the Spanish-speaking and the Indians, the latter being about eighteen different tribes.

We have wanted to translate the Bible into the native tongue. It is a difficult language. Many sounds are different from anything either in English or Spanish. But with the help of signs we have made out some of these sounds.

The dialects have very nice distinctions. We must determine whether the woman who touched Christ's garment grasped it, stroked it, or just brushed it. On the other hand, many words are lacking. The word "glory" is without equivalent. So it is with "confession" and "Savior." We have been able to make a first translation of the gospels of Mark and Luke. They will need many revisions. But a beginning has been made in the needy work of bringing God's Word to the people of Guatemala in their own tongue.

Mrs. Kitty Cox,
wife of the Rev. Newberry Cox,
Missionaries to Guatemala.

STANDING FOR CHRIST IN BUSINESS

By Allan C. Emery
Boston Wool Merchant, Wheaton College Trustee

There is always something incomplete to me in a stirring appeal that young people go to the ends of the earth to uphold the message of the cross. I long to hear an appeal to young men and women who do not feel led to go to the foreign field and who for many reasons may not be able to offer themselves in full-time Christian service at home. They may be called to the great task of standing for Christ in the business world.

I really believe it is harder, many times, for young men and women to stand alone for Christ in the business world than it is for young people on the mission field where they have some measure of Christian fellowship.

Many times a young Christian stenographer is working in an office with a superior who is unworthy of her; and a Christian young man often has to stand his ground and make his moral and spiritual decisions when all his business associates are against him. To remain true to Christ and sweet tempered is no easy task, but Christ will hold him fast.

The business world needs to feel the impact of the Christian way of doing things!

I believe that every last person should be urged to carry the gospel to the four corners of the earth. But if God does not carry you there, and you make business your life work, don't let the light of the gospel grow dim and fade away.

Before the last World War, Viscount Grey, seeing from his London window a lamp-lighter making his nightly rounds, said, "The lights are going out tonight all over Europe, and they will not be lighted again in my time."

Don't let the light go out in your heart! You here at Wheaton know how to hold Him fast. There are graduates whose lights have gone out or grown dim. It is easy to slip. It is easier to go with the tide or the current than against it. But you will never have to give up with God on your side! Whatever you learn, know this: that by the grace of God you will never fail in the truest sense.

Remember in the days ahead the story of the last breakfast. Three times our Lord asked Peter: "Lovest thou me?" If you, too, will love Him "more than these," you may be a Peter and have your Pentecost.

It may be far harder to stand for Christ in the business world than in darkest Africa. But whatever career or profession you choose, by the grace of God you can let your light shine and win souls for Him.

During a war some years ago, a surgeon, while probing for a bullet in a drummer boy, asked him, "Does it hurt?" He said, "No matter, doctor. You probe deep enough and you'll find the Emperor." Someone is going to probe deep in your life some day. Will you be able to say, "Probe deep enough, and you will find the Emperor, Christ my King!"

Let us dare to be Daniels for Christ; let us dare to stand alone in the business world or wherever our lot may be cast, and may our light never go out. May it be a light that shineth more and more unto the perfect day!

LOOKING FORWARD AND BACKWARD

THE GLORY OF HIS GRACE

God's choice of us in Christ was more primal than His founding of the universe. He planned this before He designed the fair cosmos, laid out the orbits of the planets and the courses of the stars, yea, before He created the angelic hosts. Salvation was His first thought: our salvation, my salvation. The only explanation of our being in Christ is that we are His chosen ones.

God did not make an eternal choice of us just to have us live tolerably decent lives. God chose us to live uncommon lives, lives whose only explanation is His triumphant grace. The goal and purpose of God in our lives is to give expression to the life of Jesus Christ. The whole divine, eternal movement is fraught with fulness of blessing for our lives, that we might be carried along in the train of His triumph and that the aroma of the King's palace and garden might be shedding heavenly fragrance wherever we go and the divine attributes of the Son of God be manifested through the spiritual graces of our Christian characters.

DR. WILLIAM H. WRIGHTON,
chairman, Department of Philosophy,
University of Georgia.

LOOKING FORWARD AND BACKWARD

By Dr. V. Raymond Edman, Ph. D.
Acting President, Wheaton College

THE WORD January has a pagan origin. The ancient Roman deity Janus was represented by two opposite faces, symbolizing the two faces of a door. Janus looked both forward and backward. Likewise, at the beginning of a new year, let us look in both directions.

In looking backward, let us go to distant and remote years in the history of the college.

I have been greatly blessed by reading the life of the late Charles Albert Blanchard. A small portion of that reading I wish to share with you today, with emphasis on some of the spiritual values therein for the present hour.

To many of us, the name of Charles A. Blanchard is just another name; to others it stands for a great man who lived a life of prayer in every detail of his great life.

Dr. Blanchard learned early that God answers prayer. His first experience was a heart-warming one. He was about twelve years of age. Someone had given him a knife, and one day, while he was playing, he lost it. He knew that a knife lost in the grassy commons, as a usual thing, would never be found. He had been playing over an acre of ground. There was no chance to find it even by sheer providence. But he wanted the knife. So, he writes, "I knelt by my bed and asked God to direct me to the knife." Rising, he went down to the corner, walked two blocks one way and two another and saw his knife.

"I could not have walked more directly or quickly to it," he writes. "Now this would seem to many the height of foolishness. The inference that God answers prayer will be doubted. But I am not now an advocate; I am a witness to something that actually happened."

There are some other chapters of Dr. Blanchard's life that hold timely lessons for us all.

"In public life," he writes, "I was thrown into constant opposition to the world, the flesh, and the devil. . . . . . Many a time I have gone into a town to begin work and after all arrangements had been made as best I could make them, I have gone to a cemetery or a bit of woods outside of town and, all alone with God, kneeled down and talked with Him. . . . . In times of danger I have been marvelously kept in body, soul, and spirit.

"In my college work, I have had the same spirit. The college was poor, some would say that it was desperately poor; one small building, practically no endowment and the hatred and animosity of all wicked people who knew what we were trying to do. Along with this indifference was the fear of many good people who knew what we were attempting. What combination of circumstances could be much more difficult than this?

"I made many mistakes; but I never made the mistake of being careless about the real interests of my fellowmen. In some small measure God did enable me to desire that things should be right, that all people should have a chance, that the poor and ignorant should not be trampled down by the powerful and unscrupulous; and *in all these years of labor, I learned to pray.* I kept on learning, and although I am sure thousands of God's dear children have prayed more believingly, abundantly, and successfully than I, nevertheless I shall praise God through all eternity that He taught me to pray as well as He did, and because I received from Him so many things in answer to prayer that I certainly did not merit, and that I, myself, have no reason to believe that I should otherwise have obtained."

In that one sentence—"in all these years of labor, I learned to pray"—I find spiritual eloquence and spiritual fire.

I am reminded of the words in Luke 17:5: "And the apostles said unto the Lord, Increase our faith. And the Lord said, If ye had faith as a grain of mustard seed, ye might say unto this sycamine tree, Be thou plucked up by the root, and be thou planted in the sea; and it should obey you."

What is our Lord teaching us here regarding prayer? I think we put the emphasis frequently in the wrong place. He recognized that the faith of the disciples was small because they themselves said, "Increase our faith." But then He answered and said, "If ye had faith as a grain of mustard seed." Here He does not place His emphasis on the smallness of the faith but on the vitality of that faith. If He had chosen something small, He might have said, "as a grain of sand or a speck of dust." But, no, He chose something living. He said, "If your faith were as a grain of mustard seed." It is not because of the size of our faith in our eyes or in God's eyes, rather the real question is whether it is a living faith.

Our Lord said of the smallest seed that in that seed is contained the promise of life. If it be sown and tended, out of it will come root, stalk, branch, flower, and fruit. Out of it will come beauty and fruitfulness and usefulness—all these are contained in that seed. Therein is the real criterion of faith: does it believe God, trust, and obey Him? Or is it merely a very small but human faith, dead and inert like a grain of sand? One might

plant grains of sand, water and tend them, but these will
never grow.

There is, then, a dynamic faith and a static faith. The
faith that is static does not act upon the promise. But a
dynamic faith will take God's promise for itself and will
believe that God who made the promise will not fail to
bring it to pass.

We remember that little ship, tossed by storm, upon
which Paul stood. All human hope of being saved was
gone. However, Paul knew that the Lord had stood by
him and had assured him that not only would he be
saved but also all on board. On the deck of that storm-
tossed ship stood a single man who could say to those
cowed sailors, "Be of good cheer, for *I believe God* that
it shall be even as it was told unto me."

What tremendous living faith in the promise of God!
So we say, "Lord, increase our faith." If ye have a living
faith like that of Charles A. Blanchard and Paul, to
believe God, then you say, "All this, God has done for
me."

> *There is a place where thou canst touch the eyes*
> *Of blinded men to instant, perfect sight;*
> *There is a place where thou canst say, "Arise,"*
> *To dying captives, bound in chains of night;*
> *There is a place where thou canst reach the store*
> *Of hoarded gold and free it for the Lord.*
> *There is a place—upon some distant shore—*
> *Where thou canst send the worker or the Word,*
> *Where is that blessed place—dost thou ask, "Where?"*
> *O Soul, it is the secret place of prayer.*

THE CALL TO MISSIONARY SERVICE

WANTED: SOUL-WINNERS IN AFRICA

This is the jubilee year of our work in South Africa. Fifty golden years in service have been given us by the Lord.

It was through the work of Andrew Murray that our work began. He prayed the South African General Mission into existence. Today, we work in a dozen different countries. Today, all across this section of Africa, there is a chain of light, the Light of the world.

In Portuguese East Africa are three million souls in darkness. This is the largest unevangelized portion of Africa south of the equator. They are waiting for an ambassador for Christ. Three million souls are waiting for some of you to carry to them the story of Calvary's cross. There is a field of need in that far-flung continent, a field in need of a God-sent winner of souls.

THE REV. ARTHUR BOWEN,
South African General Mission.

THE CALL TO MISSIONARY SERVICE

By Dr. Charles Ernest Scott, D. D.
Missionary to China, Father of the late Betty Scott Stam

Young people, I desire earnestly your largest usefulness for God. The wise man associates himself as far as he can with the noblest and most meaningful enterprises. The most important thing in life is that which most concerned the Lord Jesus—getting Himself made known savingly among men. This was the central theme of His life.

The burden of proof rests on us to show God a good reason—one that He, as the God of reason will accept—why we do not go to the neediest field we can fill. On general principles, that is incontestibly the foreign field.

I suggest some of the things that constitute a call to missionary work. The challenge to us is that everyone should go to the neediest work unless deterred by some reason God will accept as a good one.

One factor of importance is *our youth*. Old people have lost their opportunity. We need youth with health. And, of course, we need the highest education with all the possible attainments we can command. Whatever capability you possess, God will use to a larger extent on the foreign field than it could ever be used at home. You don't dry up on the foreign field.

Take as an example Dr. Fitch, who was a printer. Coming to China, he at once began printing tracts in Chinese. He gathered around him Christian boys and other helpers and established a commercial press. Today this enormous business prints a great number of books and text-books for China, with colored charts and maps.

This is but one aspect of his fruitful life, for Dr. Fitch had many other interests in pressing for the kingdom of God.

You know also that the *great need* is another element in the call. Consider the numerical vastness of the need. Millions and millions do not mean much to you. Think instead, of traveling on the great highways of China for ninety-four days and meeting only one mission station. Our work alone covers some twelve counties, with only my honored colleague, R. A. Torrey and I, as evangelistic missionaries. I view the need from my own personal experience. Counting villages from hilltops in my field, there are fifty villages in only one section that I have never entered. Those villages are calling to you. The only generation you can reach is *this* generation.

Think not merely of the vastness of the need, but of the *spiritual intensity* of this need. Let me suggest the lovelessness, the lostness, the homelessness, the helplessness, the hopelessness of those without Christ. Think of the need for brotherly love. In Canton, during one year, more than sixteen hundred fifty times did the invading planes go over in waves, sometimes butchering in a single day two thousand women and girls. That gives you an idea of the appalling need for Christ in the hearts of men, butchering civilian populations in fiendish glee.

In my travels in the States, I have found towns with five hundred to one thousand people and ten preachers in as many churches ministering to gospel-hardened hearts. But think of the waiting millions of the Far East alone. They must wait until we take the gospel to them. Remember Paul's great questions: "How then shall they call on Him in Whom they have not believed? And how shall they believe in Him of Whom they have not heard? And how shall they hear without a preacher? And how shall they preach, except they be sent?" (Rom. 10:15.)

In the early years of my evangelistic ministry, as I was preaching in the market, an old man pushed forward and said: "If all you say is true, why did you not come a long time ago and tell us about Christ?" Can we answer that? In God's sight, we shall have to answer it. A million a month are passing into Christless graves in China. While we make one million converts, a hundred million pass into Christless graves. At that rate, we can overtake the church's main mission as soon as we can build a bridge from Mars to the moon.

Still another element in the call is our professed *love for Christ*. "Why call ye me Lord, Lord, and do not the things I ask of you?" It seems cowardice to take Christ as Savior from the power and penalty and punishment of our sins and not at the same time take Him as Lord of our lives, to command us as He will. Do you take Him as the Lord of your life?

Mark well our Lord's four tremendous "alls." He said: *"All power* is given unto me in heaven and in earth. Go ye therefore, and teach *all nations,* baptizing them in the name of the Father, and of the Son, and of the Holy Ghost; teaching them to observe *all things* whatsoever I have commanded you: and, lo, I am with you *all the days,* even unto the end of the world" (Matt. 28:18-20). God's command is a categorical imperative. His being always with us, you notice, is the promise dependent on our going. If we do His will, He is with us.

Many Christians give the impression that their lives are too precious to be poured out for Christ. We need to realize that this call is a man's job. If we have the courage and the wisdom to risk all for Him, He gives us all we need for the undertaking. In His infinite wisdom and power, motivated by His infinite love, He gives us what, in His judgment, is best for us.

I think the greatest impression made on my daughter, Betty Scott Stam, came to her in Egypt. In the sarcophagus of Rameses II, we saw a bowl of wheat which was to go with the great conqueror into the spirit world. If that bowl of wheat had only been sown through the years, we mused, how many tons of wheat there might have been to feed the starving millions of China! Have you the courage, the wisdom, and the daring thus to sow the seed of your life for Christ?

"They that be wise shall shine as the brightness of the firmament; and they that turn many to righteousness as the stars for ever and ever" (Dan. 12:3). This verse my mother taught me when I was a boy.

May I suggest the *fruitfulness* of such a life *here* and *now?* One of our first generation missionaries of our Presbyterian Mission in Shantung province of North China had forty million souls for his parish. He went years ago to a certain village and carried there, for the first time, the story of Jesus. Those people became Christians and Christian workers and markedly used for Christ in many parts of China. In that village the missionary laid his hand on the head of a little boy and said, "I am going to pray God that some day you will become a minister of the gospel." That little boy became the Rev. Ting Limer, the greatest Chinese evangelist. In his ministry, he won many college students to Christ. His life in its fruitfulness was like that of the Apostle John. This episode was but one of many in the life of Dr. Hunter Corbett that went out in waves of blessed fruitfulness for his master, Christ.

May each of you settle this question for yourself now. With God's help, may you make a wise decision as to whether He is calling you.

THE BIBLE'S MOST IMPORTANT
COMMAND

LIGHT AND DARKNESS IN CHINA

China is the oldest civilized nation. One reason it has existed so long is that it has obeyed the command, "Honor thy father and mother."

China can claim one-fourth of John 3:16, for China is supposed to have one-fourth of the world's population. Then heaven should be one-fourth Chinese. But alas, it is not so. Do you know there is only one Chinese Christian in a thousand?

However, there is a bright side. China is a land of opportunity. Last year the British Foreign Missionary Society sold more Bibles and Christian books in China than in any other nation in the world. In a single day in Chungking, the war capital, more Bibles had been sold than in any one year before the war. In Shanghai, we have a radio broadcasting station devoted solely to preaching the gospel.

There are three kinds of missionaries. The go-missionaries hear the call and go to the field to gather the harvest; the co-missionaries cannot go but co-operate at home by prayer and gift; the o-missionaries neither go, nor pray, nor have any burden at all for the spread of the gospel.

LELAND WANG,
Chinese evangelist.

THE BIBLE'S MOST IMPORTANT COMMAND

By Dr. Oswald J. Smith, D. D., F. R. G. S.
Hymn-Writer; Pastor, The People's Church, Toronto
Speaker at Mid-Winter Evangelistic Services

HERE IS a message for those only who want God's best for their lives. The text for such a message you will find in the familiar words of Eph. 5:18, "Be filled with the Spirit."

This is, in the first place, a command. I think it is the most important command in the Word of God. The commands of Moses are known to the ends of the earth, but I do not look upon those commands as more important than this one. Likewise, there is the command to be baptized, but that is not as important as to "be filled with the Spirit." For when we have obeyed this command, we shall have obeyed every other command; we shall have met every requirement of the divine law.

This command was given to one of the most spiritual churches of the early Christian era. Had it been given to the Corinthian church, we might have understood more readily, but it was given to the Ephesian church, and if it was necessary for the Christians at Ephesus, how much more necessary it is for our apostate church today!

I have visited hundreds of churches in all parts of the world. The most spiritual of those, to my mind, was the Russian church in Paris. Yet I could stand before that congregation of Russian Christians and exhort them to "be filled with the Spirit." And if I could say that to them, then those words will find a meaningful place in any church anywhere in the world. Paul's message today to every church, were he to come back, would be epitomized well in these words. Paul would say to every church, "Be filled with the Spirit."

In every Christian group and in every church there are some filled and some not filled with the Spirit. If you would be led into the fullness of the Spirit, your problems would be more or less solved, for you would know what God wants you to do in the situations that confront you. The divine purpose would be open to you.

I am going to answer two questions: "How may I be filled with the Spirit?" and "How may I know that I am filled?"

There are four conditions that suggest themselves as I study the Word of God, as prerequisites for being filled with the Spirit. There must be confession, renunciation, surrender, belief.

You will never get anywhere with God until you confess your sins. And if you confess your sins, He is faithful and just to forgive you your sins and to cleanse you from all unrighteousness. Sins confessed are sins forgiven. Not only so, but apart from confession there is no spiritual blessing. We shall plead in vain for the Spirit's power if we do not confess.

I am not speaking along doctrinal lines, but I am being practical. Is there some hidden sin, something you are harboring, something you will not confess to God? Does something stand between you and spiritual blessing?

There are three kinds of confession. First, there is private confession. If your sin has been committed against God, confess it only to God. But if your sin has been personal, then you will find it necessary to go to your brother and make the wrong right and possibly even to make restitution if that is required for a full confession. Then there is public confession. If your sin has been against society—if it is a sin everybody knows about—there must be public confession. Remember that to be wrong with man is to be wrong with God. We cannot walk with God and refuse to walk with our fellow-men.

Sin must not only be confessed, but it must be renounced. Our confessions are valueless and useless unless we renounce our sins. It isn't a question of committing a sin, confessing it, then going again and committing it; confession must include renunciation. You may get victory over most of your sins, but that is not sufficient: your besetting sin may still remain. Unless you get victory over that sin, your life will be wrecked. But you say, "I can't break away from my sin." Listen! Are you *willing* to forsake your sin? More than that, are you *determined* to forsake your sin? You say, "Of course, all Christians are!" Ah, no; some love their sins! If you are not willing to forsake your sins, ask God to make you willing.

Do you mean business? Are you in dead earnest? You must put determination into your willingness. The prodigal son said, "I will arise and go back to my father and home."

Remember, your besetting sin will follow you all your life. And it is the little foxes that spoil the vines!

The third step in the Spirit-filled life is surrender. Renunciation is negative; surrender is positive. You are not your own; you are bought with a price. You must be willing, therefore, to do anything God wants you to do, go anywhere He wants you to go.

For three dollars I once bought a broncho from a man who was going to shoot it because the animal was ill. I nursed the broncho back to health and eventually sold it for forty dollars, a good bargain. But while the broncho was mine, he never had a bit or bridle on him. He wasn't broken, but was absolutely wild and untamed. He belonged to me, but I couldn't ride him because he wasn't broken.

How many of you have never been broken? We are of no use to God. We wonder why we are set aside. It is just because we are not broken. We are not fit for the Master's use. We want to choose for ourselves, go our own way. We have never recognized another as Master.

We have never known what it is to have someone take over the reins and say, "Here I am, your Master, taking charge of you." No; our wills must be broken; for unless you and I are willing to meet these conditions, we are going to be valueless in the eyes of God. We must surrender our proud wills, our wayward spirits, to His guiding hand. Let us come, saying, "Master, here am I."

But what about faith? What about believing? Don't worry about faith. The moment you confess sin, renounce it, and surrender to God, faith will be the easiest thing in the world.

Are you willing to pay the price to take these steps? Do you want to be used of God? Do you look at others who are being used, wondering why you are not? Are you willing to pay the price that they have paid, to go the way they have gone?

I ask you, are you willing, are you determined to get right with God now? Confess your sins; renounce them; forsake them; be through with them! It will be easier for you to take that stand now, young people, than ten years from now. Yield wholeheartedly to the Lord Jesus Christ. Recognize that you are not your own, but that you have a Master, the Lord Jesus. Say from your heart of hearts, this moment: "Take the world but give me Jesus."

HIS ETERNAL POWER AND GODHEAD

THE REFRESHING WATER OF LIFE

"I will give unto him that is athirst of the fountain of the water of life freely . . . . Let him that is athirst come. And whosoever will, let him take the water of life freely" (Rev. 21:6; 22:17b).

Have you ever been thirsty? One night during the Meuse-Argonne drive in France, we ran out of water. The soldiers I was with did not know where water could be found. They asked me what to do. I had been carrying two canteens to have water to give to wounded men, but a piece of shell had gone through one and my other canteen was empty. It had been raining two days before. We came to a mud puddle in the road. I tried to encourage the men to forget their fears. "Here is plenty of water," I said with a laugh, and I got down and drank some of the muddy stuff.

The point of this story is that drinking muddy water, even under those circumstances, was a very foolish thing to do. We were not perishing. We were too impatient. Clean, chlorinated water was provided the next morning. Do not be satisfied with the muddy waters of this world's pleasures. The Christian message assures us that God has provided the refreshing water of life.

Dr. J. Oliver Buswell,
Former President of Wheaton College.

HIS ETERNAL POWER AND GODHEAD

By Dr. Elsie Storrs Dow, Litt. D.
Former Chairman, English Department
Wheaton College

"The voice said, Cry. And he said, What shall I cry? All flesh is grass, and all the goodliness thereof is as the flower of the field: the grass withereth, the flower fadeth: because the spirit of the Lord bloweth upon it: surely the people is grass. The grass withereth, the flower fadeth: but the word of our God shall stand forever" (Isa. 40:6-8).

The ephemeral and the eternal: man's little hour on earth; his fragile tenure, feeble hold on life: and the lastingness, the everlastingness of that which God hath spoken! The antithesis is hardly here for its own sake! But when with Miss Reese we consider life and its few years,

> *A wisp of fog between us and the sun,*

many voices join in that "cry" in both sacred and secular literature. James asks the question, "What is your life?" and answers, "Even a vapor that appeareth for a little and then vanisheth away." In darker mood, Richard II declares that death allows the king a "breath" in which to "monarchize":

> *Infusing him with self and vain conceit*
> *As if this flesh which walls about our life*
> *Were brass impregnable, and humored thus,*
> *Comes at the last, and with a little pin,*
> *Bores through his castle wall, and farewell, king!*

91

And Wolsey's "long farewell to all his greatness" reads:

> *This is the estate of man—*
> *Today he puts forth the tender leaves of hope*
> *Tomorrow blossoms—*
> *The third day brings a frost, a killing frost—*

All this is salutary enough in its place but surely not the thought in this great passage from Isaiah, whose dominant note is "Comfort ye, comfort ye my people, saith your God."

The second term of the antithesis is on a different level and might well be the insistent cry demanded from the prophet. We may at least note that the book we rightly call the Word of God *has* stood for almost two thousand years in its finished form—most of it much longer—in spite of determined effort in high places, scholastic and political, to discredit or destroy it; and stands today stronger than ever. The very latest word from the Universities of Utrecht and Amsterdam is that the documentary theory, the bulwark of the negative criticism of the Old Testament in our generation, has utterly fallen. Well, it is quite possible! It is not written that the word of the critic shall stand forever!

I gave a three minute broadcast to the alumni last winter on this subject provoked by one of three letters coming directly one after another in the so-called Educational and Religious Section of a great Chicago daily. Presumably they might be considered as fair samples of current Biblical criticism, deserving to be framed or bottled in some preservative as such.

One letter set forth that the popularity of the Bible proved nothing. The answer was and is of course that it is the *permanent* popularity of a book that counts. If it proves lasting, it is literature! The classic comes to stay! But not, therefore, to compete successfully with the popular favorite. *Gone with the Wind* is probably destined to the fate suggested by the title, but in the meantime, it outsells *Paradise Lost*. And this illustrates the all but universal law. But there is one exception: just one. In our day of prodigious sales for the book of the hour, this Book of the Ages, two thousand years old, outdistances, far outdistances, the best of the best sellers year after year. By this test as by every other true test, the Bible stands alone, in a class by itself.

I can merely suggest other tests, such as the translation into other languages. Where Shakespeare stands high with forty to his credit: *Pilgrim's Progress* and *Holy Living and Holy Dying* (by the same author) stand higher, reaching the hundred mark: the Bible of course stands the highest by far, existing in a thousand tongues, many of them recreated to receive it.

Aristotle's tests have not been superseded—unity, truth, and what Arnold translates as high seriousness. Unity is difficult—even in the shortest composition! It is so easy to cover up the *thing* said by the *things* said that the theme "or the truth revealed" is sought for oftener than found. That unity should characterize a book made up of sixty-six different books, by almost half as many different authors, extending in its composition over fifteen hundred years, written in different forms and with individual styles, is pronounced impossible, and with man it is impossible. But the miracle is wrought. The story of man's redemption is the theme stamped on the whole and every part of the whole.

There is no need to speak of the "high seriousness" of such a work; but what of its truth? We have a work-a-day definition, conformity to fact, which does well enough if we have in mind simply the reporting of facts

—things done or made. History is the report of things done and history has constantly to be rewritten. In our day the earliest records are the latest news. But though it is in Bible lands primarily that we are digging up ancient history, the Bible stands unshaken. Many of its statements, stoutly denied by critics, are confirmed; many dark passages explained; but there is no refutation of any of its records.

But truth is not conformity to facts. Facts are true or false as they conform to a higher than they. The building must conform to the blueprint; the blueprint to the thought of the architect; which brings us at once to the "one great thing in the universe"—thought. But not your thought or mine! Truth is His Who said: "As the heavens are higher than the earth, so are My ways higher than your ways, and My thoughts than your thoughts." Truth is in this Book or nowhere.

But the force of this passage is not in the withering grass and fading flowers that picture man's life on the earth, nor even in the eternal Word of God as such, nor in the contrast between the two. It is in the vital relation between them. It is to be found in the immediate context and in the wider context of the whole Scripture, and also in the implication of the Word itself. For the "Word of our God was spoken to man, and for man," and in this fact lies what we may call, in Ruskin's phrase, "the revocation of the edict of destiny." God's might is opposed to man's weakness. It makes available for man's need the wisdom and righteousness and power of the eternal God. It reveals the mind of God, the heart of God, and purpose of God, toward those whom He would redeem as His people, the sheep of His pasture. The passage quoted is almost immediately followed by the words, "He shall feed His flock like a shepherd: He shall father the lambs with His arm, and carry them in His bosom." It is preceded by the words, "The glory of the Lord shall be revealed, and all flesh shall see it together." It is followed by the injunction to Zion to Jerusalem: "Get thee up into the high mountain . . . . lift up thy voice with strength . . . say unto the cities of Judah, Behold your God!"

But the glory of the Lord revealed to Isaiah in a vision and to us through his cry is God's provision for man in the gift of His Son as the new Head of our race; the second Adam, not as merely a living soul, but as a life-giving Spirit—life-giving, too, in the complete sense of giving His life a ransom for many. For as representative of the race whose headship He assumes, He assumes its guilt and pays the penalty of its transgressions with His blood. But He conquers death and in His life we, too, have life, and life forevermore. To the age-long, world-wide question, "If a man die, shall he live again?" there comes no answer save in Christ's words, "Because I live, ye shall live also." Through this Word of our God, we, too, shall stand forever.

We may reason with Tennyson:

> *My own dim life should teach me this,*
> *That life must live forevermore,*
> *Else earth were darkness at the core*
> *And dust and ashes all that is!*

But how are we to know that "earth is not darkness at the core, and dust and ashes all that is"? By this, that the truth is here and the life is here in Him Who was "both the truth and the life" or it is nowhere.

John writes, "The Word was made flesh and dwelt among us and we beheld His glory." And when we question when and where and how, the reply we make

is, "On the mount of transfiguration." But Peter saw
Him by the seaside in the miraculous draft of fishes, even
His eternal power and Godhead. Much he cared for the
fishes, thrifty fisherman though he was! He saw all
that Isaiah beheld when he saw the Lord high and lifted
up and was affected in exactly the same way. Contrast
that scene with the account of the sequel to the miracle
(sign) of the feeding of the five thousand given in John's
gospel. The crowd sought Him the next morning,
finally crossing the sea in their search. He met them
with a rebuff which should have been a warning. "Ye
seek me not because ye saw the sign"—they hadn't—
"but because ye did eat of the loaves and were filled."
And in spite of His warning, we hear them presently
telling Him that Moses did this sort of thing every day!
Even saying to Him, "What sign showest thou that we
should believe thee?" And what sign can be shown
when the significance is not discerned? They had seen
no sign, no Lord! They had simply seen a great possible advantage to "themselves." But "this is the work
of God, that ye believe on Him whom He hath sent."
"As many as received Him, to them gave He power to
become the sons of God, even to them that believe on
His name."

Faith is not credulity, much less superstition. It is
the one cure for that! It is seeing the invisible by the
things that are made, even His eternal power and Godhead. It is the most powerful thing in the world.

At the feast of Cana, Jesus' mother saw and pitied the
embarrassment of their host and knew exactly what to
do about it. She found her Son and said, "They have
no wine." Some people see a rebuff in His reply. I
almost wish I could! He certainly did not say, as I have
heard preachers declare, that the time had come for a

change in their relations, or as a great commentator says that when He began to work miracles, it would be at the behest of His heavenly Father, not His earthly mother! But He did say, "You are asking for a miracle. My time for that has not yet come." Meantime His earthly mother gave directions to the servants to do as He told them to do. And His time for working miracles came then and there! How the invisible things of His thirty beautiful years, so almost completely a blank to us, except as we read them between the lines of this story, are clearly seen! His actions had compelled His mother's faith. His mother's faith compelled His action here—His beginning of miracles!

But Jesus left the Jewish lands just once, seemingly for complete rest from the crowds. But a mother in this foreign country took the chance of a life-time to seek His help for her afflicted daughter. This time we have the rebuff in its sharpest form. He not only told her truly that He was not sent but to the lost sheep of the house of Israel but that it was not meet to take the children's bread and cast it to the dogs! She replied with the wisdom of the serpent and the innocent softness of the dove, "But the little dogs eat of the crumbs that fall from the Master's table, Lord!" And Jesus said, "O woman, great is thy faith—be it unto thee even as thou wilt." Jesus was the greatest of artists as well as the greatest of teachers. He knew how to give the strike, or blow, the finishing touch that brings from the beautiful thing the perfection of beauty. He had for once left His own country for the sake of rest. I think He found it in the faith of this woman. I am not sure that He did not go for just that—it was worth it.

Lord Bacon's explanation of the inability of many scientists to see God in the "things that are made" is that they do not see that they *are* made. They ask not "why," but "how," and build up a system. And then they worship the system, not the Creator. They worship the work of their own hands, and "professing themselves to be wise, they become fools." Paul says they "were without excuse." But the people of Jesus' day *saw* the things that were done by Him, things "which none other man did"; and He said that "they have no cloak for their sin." They "have both seen and hated both me and my Father."

But they had not yet seen what we have seen. They crucified Him and He rose from the dead. He clearly instructed His disciples to testify to these two facts as "written" and as witnessed by themselves and to preach repentance and the remission of sins to all nations beginning at Jerusalem (Luke 24:45-48). How closely Peter adhered to these instructions we see at Pentecost and in all his subsequent preaching. From this great beginning, this little band of humble disciples went out to change the face of the world. That world called itself Christendom and dated its documents from His birth, the "year of our Lord." But the work so gloriously begun is still unfinished. The instructions are unchanged. The call to repentance must still be sounded forth, and our lips and lives—transformed lives—must still show forth His death and the power of His resurrection. We are His workmanship in Christ Jesus; and in this supreme work of His hands, men will see His eternal power and Godhead. "They overcame him by the blood of the Lamb and by the word of their testimony, and they loved not their lives unto the death."

THE TECHNIQUE OF
PERSONAL WORK

CARRYING THE GOSPEL TO THE MONKS

There is a work beginning among the Catholic Church in Chile. The monks are hungry for the Word. Many of them have come out of the Church. One young monk, called George Jordan, has come out for the Lord and is now learning what persecution means.

One day I found a New Testament in Spanish. It had been translated from the original Greek by a monk. He sent the manuscript to Rome without a word of Catholic doctrine in it. It was not examined carefully and was passed and stamped with the ecclesiastical approval. I have sold this Testament to scores of young monks who can read here the unadulterated truth of the gospel. I also have been able to preach to the monks all over Chile.

Will you pray for our work in Chile? We need laborers. Will you pray that they that live in darkness shall see a great light?

—THE REV. W. M. STRONG,
Soldiers and Gospel Mission, Chile.

THE TECHNIQUE OF PERSONAL WORK

By the Rev. Martin Luther Long, D. D.
Minister, First Baptist Church, Burbank, Cal.

The recent condition of the church, both in numerical and spiritual strength, is cause for serious apprehension, to say the least. After an unbiased survey of the ordinary evangelistic campaign, some are convinced that the day of mass evangelism is over. Especially is this true in America. It is also to be lamented that an increasingly small fraction of professing Christians ever make any personal effort to win a lost soul to Christ.

There are of course reasons for this situation, the foremost of which is the fact that many professing Christians are merely refined pagans without the slightest conception of what it really means to be alive from the dead. Another cause of spiritual decline is the fact that even among those who have been born from above, the experiences of personal work have been discouraging, and I think largely because many of us have become the victims of false and erroneous teaching on this vital subject. For instance, I myself have been taught that the way to approach an individual regarding his soul's salvation is simply to quote a liberal amount of Scripture. But when I began to study the methods of the New Testament, I soon discovered that what I had been taught was entirely unscriptural. In First Corinthians 2:14, we read, "But the natural man receiveth not the things of the Spirit of God: neither can he know them because they are spiritually discerned." To approach, therefore, the "natural man," i.e., an ordinary pagan, with some remote passage of Scripture is just about as inconsistent as praying for the dead.

Now let us turn to the fourth chapter of John and study the method of Jesus in winning a lost soul. We notice at the very outset that Christ loved people, all people. He gave His best to the worst, and the woman of Samaria was one of the worst.

Notice His approach, "Give me a drink." He did not quote a single verse of Scripture. He did not intimate that she was wicked and He was righteous. He did not talk about God and the devil or heaven and hell. Had He done so, she would have reacted to Him precisely as people reacted to us when we foolishly approached them with an air of religious finality. Our Lord made His approach by talking about the commonplace things of life: things the common individual can understand; things in which the common individual is interested. At the moment this woman of Samaria was interested in water, so Christ talked about water, then living water, then fountains of water that spring up into everlasting life. In other words, Jesus would discover the dominant interest in people and lead them along the line of that interest to their need of salvation.

In college, some students are interested in ideas, theories, and facts. Some are interested in athletics. Others pursue another line of interest. But whatever the interest, we must discover it and from that interest lead the individual to the supreme interest—Christ.

But we must not deceive ourselves. Winning folk to Christ, even when we use the method of Jesus, is no work for a novice, or easy task. For the past two thousand years, so-called Christians have grossly misrepresented Christ, and as a result a mere reference to the Christian religion precipitates an attitude of skepticism on the part of many.

People will begin to raise issues. The Samaritan woman did. "How is it that Thou, being a Jew, asketh drink of me, which am a woman of Samaria?" Of course Jesus could have conversed intelligently on the Jew-Samaritan issue, an issue which has many counter parts in our modern world. But instead, He raised a higher issue. He talked about "living water," and as He did so, she forgot all about the Jew-Samaritan problem. And right here is where the devil leads us astray. He gets us all tangled up about being a fundamentalist or a modernist, or a pre-millennialist or a post-millennialist, and before we realize it the one we would win to Christ has lost interest. The reason is we got lost in verbal pyrotechnics and theological controversies.

But the woman of Samaria was not easily won. "Art Thou greater than our father Jacob?" she asked. Comparing personalities has always been a popular escape. Of course, Jesus knew all about Jacob and could have truthfully said a good many unsavory things about him, but He was out to bring salvation to the woman and not merely to win an argument. Someone has said, "To win an argument, you need only to be clever, but to win a person, you need to be Christian." So Jesus dismissed Jacob with the words, "Whosoever drinks any of the water that I shall give him, will never, never thirst. But the water that I shall give him will become a fountain within him of water springing up for the Life of the Ages" (John 4:13, Weymouth Translation). This He said to an outcaste woman, displaying as He always did, an amazing confidence in every human being. Jesus believed in people. And if we are to realize any degree of success in the winning of men and women to Christ, we must believe in them.

The woman of Samaria, like most of us, was cursed with a divided personality. She had mixed motives. She wanted "the well of water" to relieve her of the necessity of physical exertion. In other words, she was selfish. She would accept the offer of Christ, not because of what He was, but because of what she could get out of Him. And everybody knows we have a great many well-meaning Christians going around telling people they ought to accept Christ so they can go to heaven. In other words, accept Christ for what you can get out of Him, not because of what He is, which, in the final analysis, is pure and unvarnished selfishness. "Whosoever, said Jesus, will save his life [i.e., accept Christ merely to get to heaven] shall lose it: but whosoever will lose his life for My sake, the same shall find it." "To me to live is Christ, and to die is gain," cries Paul. And his destiny he leaves with God. So when the woman of Samaria manifested the spirit of a divided personality, Christ went straight to her moral problem. There is a moral problem in every life. In some people it manifests itself in the sins of the disposition (the most heinous of all sin according to Christ), in others it manifests itself in the sins of the flesh, as in the case of the Samaritan woman. Now, what did Christ do? Did He get all excited and tell her what an awful woman she was? No, He simply led the woman to acknowledge her own sin by the simple but tender request, "Go, call thy husband, and come hither." The woman was terrified. She was brought face to face with her sins. She was quite uncomfortable and had to prepare a way of escape, so she played her last card.

She raised an abstract religious issue: "I perceive that Thou art a prophet. Our fathers worshipped in this mountain; and Ye say, that in Jerusalem is the place where men ought to worship." Obviously the Samaritan woman was religious. All people are. Religion is the greatest curse and the greatest blessing the world has ever known. How did Jesus meet this abstract religious question? By simply raising a higher issue, namely, "God is a spirit, and they that worship Him must worship Him in spirit and in truth." In the light of religious reality, Jerusalem and the mountain are soon forgotten as utterly irrelevant.

The purpose of personal work is to reveal Christ. In the light of, "I that speak unto thee am He," the woman, like the prodigal son, came to herself. She did not know the answers to the theological difficulties of her day, but once she saw Jesus, that was enough. She surrendered. And when we die to everything but the will of God, we begin to follow Christ, and in following Him, naturally we become fishers of men.

> *Have you found the heavenly Light?*
> *Pass it on.*
> *Souls are groping in the night,*
> *Daylight gone.*
> *Hold the lighted light on high,*
> *Be a star in someone's sky;*
> *He may live who else may die,*
> *Pass it on.*

LIFE AT ITS BEST

ARMISTICE DAY REFLECTIONS

The peoples of the world have lost their sense of political direction for we have discovered, to our amazement, that a pure democracy is not safe in any part of the world.

A representative democracy is safe only if it is in accord with the "ethos" of the people. By "ethos" I mean what the ancient Greeks meant when they spoke of "ethos", namely, the tastes, the habits, the customs and the opinions of the people. And no representative democracy can be safe for any people unless there is what we call "constitutional morality" among the officers of government and among the people themselves. And by "constitutional morality" I mean devotion and adherence on the part of the officers of the government to the great fundamental principles of the constitution, and a similar fidelity and devotion to the fundamental law by the people themselves.

JOHN F. VOIGHT,
President, Illinois State Bar Association.

LIFE AT ITS BEST

By Dr. H. A. Ironside, Litt. D.
Pastor, The Moody Church, Chicago

THE TEXT I HAVE IN MIND for this message is found in the Book of Genesis, chapter 27, the last seven words of verse 46: "What good shall my life do me?" You may or may not recall the connection and the circumstances under which these words were uttered. They were spoken querulously by a disgruntled mother-in-law who felt that her eldest son had made a fatal mistake in a double matrimonial venture. As Mark Twain said of Brigham Young, "He loved not wisely but too many." And they were both of such disposition that they made life unbearable for Rebecca, the wife of Isaac. She had been terribly disappointed in Esau's marriages, and she feared that Jacob might contact some heathen woman of similar type. So she exclaimed to Isaac, "If Jacob take a wife of the daughters of Heth, such as these, which are the daughters of the land, what good shall my life do me?" And so she urged Isaac to send Jacob down to her brother's home in Syria on a wife-hunting expedition. It is not my intention, however, to occupy you with the matrimonial affairs of Isaac's family. I am really doing something most homileticians consider very reprehensible. They would say I am attempting to use a text for a pretext, for it is just these seven words that I am thinking about and that I want you to consider with me at this time.

"What good shall my life do me?" Each of us may well ask himself this serious question. Life is a wonderful boon and a great privilege, if lived aright and used to the glory of God and the blessing of humanity. But it may become a terrible curse to ourselves and others if we follow the path of self-will, trample on divine precepts, refuse the grace of God, which is offered us in Christ Jesus, and live for the world, the flesh, and the devil. A perverted life is a wasted life and will leave nothing but regret behind. How true this was of Judas! Filled with wondrous privileges and glorious opportunities, he literally threw his life away, and Jesus said of him at last, "Good were it for that man if he had never been born." What good did the life of Judas do him? No good at all, but infinite harm.

Life at the best is short. Seventy or more years, and we spend them all as a tale that is told. Then the place that knew us once knows us no more forever. Happy is the man who leaves a record behind that he has lived for God and glorified Him in all his ways. You will remember the first question and answer of the Shorter Catechism of the Presbyterian Church: "What is the chief end of man?" "The chief end of man is to glorify God and to enjoy Him forever." This is indeed life at its best. You will recall Daniel's solemn words to the dissolute King Belshazzar: "The God in whose hand thy breath is, and whose are all thy ways, hast thou not glorified." He was weighed in the balances and found wanting. Life for him was an utter failure. God grant it may not be true of any of you who listen to me today.

> *Weighed in the balance and wanting,*
> *Weighed, but no Savior is there;*
> *Weighed, but thy soul has been trifling,*
> *Weighed, and found lighter than air.*

Life is worth much and yet treated as though it were worthless by many. I wonder if you have ever seen the simple little acrostic on the word "Time." It goes like this:

There is a gem of untold worth,
It's given by God to men on earth;
Millions don't prize it; so throw it away;
Eternity dawns, and it's lost for aye.

So it is with life in the case of many, many people. The life that is worth while is a Christ-centered life. The Apostle Paul said, "For me to live is Christ and to die is gain." Elsewhere he said, "Ye have died, and your life is hid with Christ in God." John says, "He that hath the Son hath life, and he that hath not the Son of God hath not life." Life with unsaved men is a mere existence and generally a very selfish existence. Life for the child of God is a glorious adventure, an unselfish devotion to the One who has redeemed us.

We have often been reminded that we pass this way but once. How important, then, to live well! Think of the many people who have lived and died and left no impression for good on anyone else! Of King Jehoram, the godless son of the godly Jehoshaphat, the man who had trampled on all his father's instruction, we read that "thirty and two years old was he when he began to reign, and he reigned in Jerusalem eight years, and departed without being desired" (II Chron. 21:20). What a solemn epitaph! The people were glad to get rid of him. They felt relieved when he had gone. Doubtless many said, "Good riddance of bad rubbish." His was a life utterly wasted. How great the contrast in the case of King David, who, whatever his failures, was a man who had judged his sins in the presence of God and sought to live for the glory of God and the good of his people! Of him we are told, "After he had served his own generation by the will of God, he fell on sleep" (Acts 13:36). That was a life worth while and an epitaph to be valued.

Think of the many brilliant and talented men and women endowed by God with remarkable gifts who have wasted their lives in sensuality, selfishness, and godlessness. One is reminded of that brilliant darling of society, Lord Byron, who, as he looked back over a wasted life, wrote:

> *My days are in the yellow life,*
> *The flower, the fruit of life is gone;*
> *The worm, the canker, and the grief*
> *Are mine alone.*

How differently he might have felt had he yielded himself to Christ and made the glory of God his first consideration!

How often we hear elderly people as they look back over the years that have gone, exclaim, "Really, life is not worth living!" How different is the story of those who have lived for God!

I trust that most of you gathered here today have already yielded your lives to Christ, but if there are those who have not yet done so, oh, let me plead with you tenderly, earnestly, seriously, do not waste another hour ere you bow in repentance at the feet of Him who is the way, the truth, and the life, and receive Him as Savior, and go forth to obey Him as Lord.

We who are saved look back with the greatest of regret on the years spent in sin. I often think of that little verse:

> *I lived for myself, for myself alone,*
> *For myself and none beside,*
> *Just as if Jesus had never lived*
> *And as if He had never died.*

But, oh, how I praise Him for ever opening my blinded eyes to see that the only life really worth living is the life yielded to Himself.

And right here let me point out that you must have life from God before you can live for Him, and that life He offers freely to all who trust His blessed Son. "He that believeth on the Son hath everlasting life." "The gift of God is eternal life through Jesus Christ, our Lord." When this life has been received, then indeed you can live a life that will be to His glory and to your own eternal joy. Do not, I beseech you, waste precious hours and days on things that do not profit, but heed the admonition of Paul to Timothy: "Lay hold on that which is really life" (I Tim. 6:19, literal translation). All else is a mirage, fleeting and evanescent, and will disappoint you at last. Consider, then, the question, "What good will my life do me?" and settle it in your heart that you will know life at its best by committing yourself to the Lord Jesus Christ and living to please Him alone.

RUNNING THE RACE TO WIN

MODERNISM GOES BACK TO EDEN

Modernism is as old as Eve. In fact, the first higher critic was the serpent, for he asked, "Yea, hath God said?"

Eve became the first doubter of God's Word, for she accepted the denial of Satan rather than the word of the Almighty.

She also became the first Unitarian, for she added to God's commandment more than He had said. God said not to eat the fruit of the tree of the knowledge of good and evil, but Eve said they were not even to touch the tree.

The devil was the first evolutionist, for he taught that by the process of natural development, we shall be as God. He not only denied the worth of God, but also the work of God.

DR. H. H. SAVAGE,
Pontiac, Mich.

RUNNING THE RACE TO WIN

THE REV. CLARENCE E. MASON, JR.
Pastor, Chelsea Baptist Church, Atlantic City, N. J.
Professor, Philadelphia School of the Bible

> *I am made all things to all men, that I might by
> all means save some. And this I do for the gospel's
> sake, that I might be partaker thereof with you. Know
> ye not that they which run in a race run all, but one
> receiveth the prize? So run, that ye may obtain. And
> every man that striveth for the mastery is temperate in
> all things. Now they do it to obtain a corruptible
> crown; but we an incorruptible. I therefore so run, not
> as uncertainly; so fight I, not as one that beateth the
> air: But I keep under my body, and bring it into sub-
> jection: lest that by any means, when I have preached
> to others, I myself should be a castaway.*
> — I COR. 9:22b-27

THERE IS NEED for this note in America today. With all of our emphasis upon athletics and care of the body, we are living in a flabby age. America has gone soft!

We walk two blocks to get our automobiles; so we can ride around the corner to a drug store. If we can't push a button and get some mechanical servant to work for us, we are irritated. In the old days, if Grandfather missed the train to the city, he said, "Too bad!" and drove back home to await the train due the next day; but today when Grandson misses a green light or one section of a revolving door, he stands in danger of an apoplectic stroke.

Yes, we are far from the pioneer endurance, despite our urgency to go places and to do things. Accompanying and checkmating all our determination is a lassitude of moral stamina, a fussiness caused by the lack of a preciseness of conviction. What pioneer daring is left has been diverted into the foolhardy channel of seeing how far we can go and yet get away with it. We are tough, but not strong; our toughness is that of a callous; we are basically soft.

In the midst of the enervating atmosphere of the present day, the value of the disciplined life, which has always moulded and shaped Christian standards of walk, is being seriously questioned and sadly undermined. Even in Christian circles, some feel we cannot stop the tide of the times but that we must reinterpret Christian standards of life to conform to the inevitable changes of our day. The denials and sacrifices of the Christian walk, they assert, succeed only in making individuals appear queer in the eyes of those they seek to win.

Let it be rung out today that if ever we who bear Christ's name should be good soldiers, with backbone and conviction, willing to endure hardness for His sake, it is now! If ever we needed those who are willing to eat at the Christian training table and to deny themselves many a tempting dainty, it is now! If ever we needed crusaders of Christian consecration and standards, in the midst of a careless age, it is now!

For our Scriptural warrant and example of the unquestionable value and superiority of the disciplined life over any other life, we look to the intimate biographical sketch the Apostle Paul gives us in the verses that have been read. His spiritual vigor and success are sufficient and soul-satisfying answer to any question concerning the worthwhileness of self-discipline.

Paul takes us in these verses on a personally conducted tour of the Greek arena, where the original Olympic games are in progress. He shows us the athletes (runners, boxers, wrestlers), the race-course, the judges' stand, the prize (the victor's wreath). Then he discusses the discipline of the body necessary victoriously to compete, and the disqualification from the prize that results from breaking the rules. As we stand by the Apostle's side, we hear him raise these thought-provoking rhetorical questions:

> *Why run the race, if not to win?*
> *Why lose the prize, and losing, sin?*
> *Why shadow box, and beat the air*
> *With ne'er a victor's wreath to wear?*
> *Why take your eyes from Christ, our goal,*
> *And enter heav'n with not one soul?*
> *Why miss the point of why we're here—*
> *With death, or Christ's return, so near?*

These solemnizing thoughts suggest three self-evident principles: Anything that is worth doing at all is worth doing rightly. Anything worth doing at all is worth doing well. Anything worth doing at all is worth doing with all our might.

The tragedy of our day is that most Christians aim at nothing and hit it every time! But no man can think on these words of the Apostle Paul and remain in doubt that the disciplined, self-denying life is the only worthwhile life, the only goal worthy of the Christian's aim.

We were once bound, he declares, but now we are free from the sin, appetites, and prejudices of the pre-conversion life. We have complete deliverance in Christ and are the servants of no man, fearing no man, but fearing God only, yet serving all men in love.

Paul made himself a servant of all, for Christ's sake, voluntarily. Having identified himself with the Master's program for the world, Paul felt no longer free to please himself. His self-imposed restrictions were not a handicap to him, he asserted. They were not a valueless series of worthless taboos nor mere slices of unnecessary liabilities, as some in our own day would have us believe. They were not just a brake on his soul. But such a life, he declared, is gain. It is gain for others and gain for self. For such a life gains more souls for Christ's kingdom. It wins the prize that endures. It is an example that assists others to run a similar race. And it avoids disqualification from the prize. That is what our rather unfortunate translation, "be a castaway," really means. Paul feared lest, even after, by his preaching, having persuaded others to run the race, he should be disqualified from the prize of the victor's crown by lack of self-discipline.

No football or basketball player is worth the space he takes on the field or court if he asks how little he can give up and still be a player. To be his best for the team, he gladly sacrifices.

Let us not, therefore, hesitate at any self-denial we must make. Let us think of how Christ denied Himself; think of what He gave up for us. For the joy of the crown that was set before Him, He endured the cross, despising the shame. And today He is on the right hand of God the Father. So let us run the race with patience, and run to win!

At this hour, "turn your eyes upon Jesus. Look full in His wonderful face. For the things of earth will grow strangely dim, in the light of Christ's glorious face!"

LIVING THE CREATIVE LIFE

MAPPING LIFE ON ETERNITY'S CHART

I wish to share with you two convictions about your life work. They may be commonplace, but they are vitally important for each.

First, every Christian ought to choose his life work in the light of the guidance and will of God. God has a plan for you. As a Christian, it is your special duty to discover that plan and to do your best to pursue it. And it will be a great source of strength to you in times of hardship if you can say to yourself, "I am in the place God wants me to be, trying my best to do the thing God wants me to do."

Second, God wants you to get the best possible preparation for the work to which He has called you. He does not want any slipshod or careless work.

Let us seek His guidance and His will and follow it implicitly in our choice of a life work, in our preparation, and in our carrying out of our life purpose after preparation is complete. Following this simple principle, students gathered here will make a contribution of incalculable value to the advance of God's kingdom on earth and to the winning of the lost to their Lord and Savior, Jesus Christ.

DR. ERNEST L. ACKLEY,
Dean of the Divinity School,
Kansas City Baptist Theological Seminary.

LIVING THE CREATIVE LIFE

By Dr. R. R. Brown, D.D.
Western District Superintendent, Christian and Missionary Alliance

In considering the matter of creative living, let us turn to the Second Book of Kings, the second chapter. There we have the words of Elijah to Elisha, "What shall I give to you?" And the response is, "I would that a double portion of Thy Spirit be upon me."

There is in these words a gripping concern over the course of living that Elisha should pursue. Every man lives either creatively or corruptly. The highest, the most noble ambition in the world today is to live creatively; not to inspire a man to be the best ball player in the world, the best student, the best musician or the finest artist, but to install a personal and vital relationship to the one great Redeemer and the gospel purpose. The world knows no higher and no more noble ambition than that motivating an individual who lives so that he will persuade men and women to come to know God as He is in Jesus Christ, the foundation of all character and all security in a man's life.

I saw a young man get up the other night before a church audience. He had a fine message, but he gave the audience the idea that he thought he was a fine preacher. The young people commented, "wonderful oratory!" You are not going out to preach, but you are going out to tell someone something. If you are dedicating your life to missionary service for Christ, the highest ambition is to make men and women come to know God as He is revealed in Christ, to know Him not only as a Savior, but also in all the fulness and revelation of His power.

The Bible is the unfolding of the person and work of Jesus Christ, and as I increase in the knowledge of the Book, I increase in the knowledge of Jesus. The youth of this generation need to be told how to be more than a success. Before we can effectively present Christ, the foundation of character and security, we need to learn how to make men and women know God. It is not sufficient merely to give information about Christ; we need also that creative impulse that make us not only articulate Him but also lead others creatively to the knowledge of Him.

There are many in our day who have a superficial method of expressing their spirituality. People get the idea that when one becomes spiritual, he must assume a superficial attitude. There was none of this in Elisha.

Elisha followed Elijah, who said, "Ask what I shall do for thee, before I be taken away from thee. And Elisha said, I pray thee, let a double portion of thy spirit be upon me." Elijah's mantle fell; Elisha picked it up, remembering the words, "If thou see me when I am taken from thee, it shall be so unto thee, but if not, it shall not be so." When the mantle fell and Elijah disappeared, Elisha turned right around to express his faith. He struck the waters of the Jordan and crossed over. He had to go to the other side of Jordan.

The place of creativeness is the other side of Jordan, the other side of Calvary. Surrender your life to His fullness. Jesus is our Elijah. He went through to the other side of Calvary. He told them to tarry, to wait, for He would drop His mantle. The Holy Spirit came.

You can walk, live, think, and act in the power of that Spirit.

THE MESSAGE OF A MOSAIC PSALM

WE SHALL BE LIKE HIM

"The heavens declare the glory of God; and the firmament showeth his handiwork" (Ps. 19:1) . . . "I will praise thee, for I am fearfully and wonderfully made" (Ps. 139:14).

We all can see the glories of the heavens, but few of us have any intimate relationship with the wonders of these mechanisms of ours.

Consider how many machines are encased in this human frame. Our bones not only hold us up, but they are hollow and are not burdensome to carry about and serve as storage space and for manufacturing body substances—a veritable factory within our skeletal structure.

But there are imperfections. The body is imperfect. The eye, for instance, is wonderfully made, but it has a blind spot and may be color blind. It is easily deluded.

Something somewhere made man imperfect in his moral and physical nature. "But we know that when He shall appear, we shall be like Him; for we shall see Him as He is" (I John 3:2). It is perfectly natural that God, Who created us, should want to see us restored to our original perfection. But nothing we can do is a means to that great spiritual end. The only means is the free gift, the atonement of Jesus Christ.

DR. GRAYSON CARROLL, M.D.,
of St. Louis, Mo., well known urologist and
Christian physician.

THE MESSAGE OF A MOSAIC PSALM

By Dr. J. Oliver Buswell, Jr., D.D., LL.D.
Former President, Wheaton College

> *Lord, Thou hast been our dwelling place in all
> generations. Before the mountains were brought forth,
> or ever Thou hadst formed the earth and the world,
> even from everlasting to everlasting, Thou art God.
> Thou turnest man to destruction; and sayest, Return,
> ye children of men. For a thousand years in Thy sight
> are but as yesterday when it is past, and as a watch
> in the night . . . For all our days are passed in Thy
> wrath: we spend our years as a tale that is told . . .
> So teach us to number our days, that we may apply
> our hearts unto wisdom . . . O satisfy us early with
> Thy mercy; that we may rejoice and be glad all our
> days . . . And let the beauty of the Lord our God
> be upon us: and establish Thou the work of our hands
> upon us; yea, the work of our hands establish Thou
> it. —* PSALM 90

HERE IN THIS famous Psalm of Moses, we have a four-fold outline: the eternity of God, the transitory character of all things human, God's eternity, which may be imparted to us, and the eternal significance of our everyday task. We can even place the last point first, for it will be pagan if we say, "Establish the work of our hands upon us." We will have builded the Tower of Babel.

"From everlasting to everlasting, Thou art God." On this verse I have spoken many times before, but I find great comfort in these words in our day of financial, spiritual, and moral chaos.

The Ninety-First Psalm seems to be the sunny result of the study of the Ninetieth Psalm.

Transitory things are a warning to us. "Thou turnest man to destruction; and sayest, Return ye children of men." God can do what we cannot. In our limited circumstances, a parent may say to his child, "Go ahead and see what happens." Not so with God. He says, "Return, ye children of men." God knows and understands, for a thousand years are as a watch in the night in His sight. The human course of affairs is likened to a flood, or to the grass that withereth by evening, or our years as a tale that is told."

If you are not really infused with Christ, if you are not resting in Him, then it will seem indeed like a tale that is told. But when you are, then all things will redound to the glory of Christ. God will put eternity in your heart, and it will not be a tale that is soon told.

Where the fear of the Lord is, is the beginning of wisdom. So teach us that life is short, that we may now accept Christ! Now is the accepted time. Today, if you will hear His voice, harden not your hearts. Let us base everything upon His grace and upon His glorious message. Upon this basis there is a definite attitude of hope toward life. In the light of the wisdom of God, Moses holds up his day's work before God.

There are two ways of looking at your life work. It is perfectly possible for a minister or a missionary to erect a Tower of Babel out of his life. But pray as Moses did that God may establish the work of your hands. We all, it is true, may have the feeling of futility, but the Lord will establish the work of our hands for eternity if we but trust in Him and put Him at the center of all we do.

THE QUESTION OF MIRACLES

THE BLESSING OF ADOPTION

How much does our adoption mean to us today? Not only have we been born again, but we have been given all the rights and privileges of sons of God. "Behold, what manner of love the Father hath bestowed upon us, that we should be called the sons of God" (I John 3:1).

We are children through the new birth, but we receive also the placement of sons. How we ought to remember our adoption when we are tempted to sin! I am a child of God. I am a son of the King.

Are we living as children of heavenly rank? Are we showing forth the virtues of Him who has called us out of darkness into His marvelous light? Are we glad, in times of distress and difficulty, that we have been made joint-heirs with Jesus Christ? All the provisions of the last will and testament of Jesus Christ have been legally possessed for us by adoption.

We are accepted, not with the Beloved but in the Beloved. The same reception is accorded me as is accorded Christ Himself. We shall go home to glory and not be in the outer circles, but we shall be in the inner circle. We shall be closer than the angels. Heaven will never cease to tell the glory of God that has been effected by our adoption as sons of God.

DR. WILLIAM H. WRIGHTON,
Chairman, Department of Philosophy,
University of Georgia.

THE QUESTION OF MIRACLES

By Dr. Harry Rimmer, D.D., Sc. D.
President, Research Science Bureau, Inc.

*This beginning of miracles did Jesus in Cana of
Galilee, and manifested forth His glory; and His
disciples believed on Him.* — John 2:11

It is a common experience for all men who enjoy an
itinerant ministry to have questions addressed to them in
campus campaigns. One of the commonest of these queries
is met at almost every meeting. When the question-box is
opened, somebody will be sure to have asked, "How do you
explain the miracles?" Every time we get that ingenuous
query, we find it difficult to restrain a tired smile. That
seems one of the silliest questions that the naive direct to
the platform.

If there is such a thing as a miracle, how can we explain
it, and if we can explain it, wherein is it miraculous? The
very word "miracle" implies an orderly procedure upon the
plane of a law higher than our present comprehension.
Exactly as this generation has learned many of the laws of
nature that were unknown to our great-grandfathers, so
also we can see that God, Who is the source of all law,
must know several things that we have not yet discovered.
When the infinite God operates in a realm that is still
superior to our knowledge, we define the result of that
operation as a miracle. Sometime ago we heard of a colored preacher whose parishioners said admiringly that he
could "unscrew the unscrutable"! We make no claims to
such amazing ability, and we deal with the miracles only

with the preconceived idea that there will be much concerning them that we shall be unable to explain until we know all things even as also we are fully known.

We cannot refrain from suggesting that this common query from student bodies is a sad evidence of an implanted infidelity. Youth is the age of faith. When we are young, we have great confidence in the future and of the place we may fill in those coming days. By the operation of faith, we are induced to invest our present in preparation for a future that is problematic, to say the least. Cynicism belongs to old age and is generally the result of drinking deep from the bitter waters of disappointment.

Without apology or equivocation, I set forth the bold statement that I have never met any measure of infidelity in a student body that was not a reflection of the attitude of some of the faculty. In the course of four years, the average student body becomes a reflection of the composite faculty. As the freshman twig is bent, the senior tree is inclined.

In an age of faith, miracles were accepted simply as they were stated. They were ascribed to God upon the simple basis that He is able. If God is able, He is also expected. It has ever seemed to us that a lack of faith in miracles must spring from an inadequate philosophy of God. Unquestionably the doubter is an exponent of the philosophy "I will not concede that God can accomplish beyond my comprehension." But if we will not admit that the Creator Whom we worship and serve is capable of performing acts and operations superior to our present comprehension, the real object of our worship becomes our own mental ability. Frankly, I must have something vastly larger than the mean limitations of my mentality as the object of my adoration.

One of the reasons I believe in God is that I am unable to comprehend Him. If I fully understood God, I would uncompromisingly reject Him. It is an old assumption that we cannot get anything into a container that is larger than that container. If God could be contained within the scope of human mentality, He would be reduced to the level of humanity. This, indeed, would be anthropomorphism.

It is conceded that one mentality cannot produce a conception that no other mentality can comprehend. It is said, for instance, that there are only twelve men in the world who thoroughly understand the Einstein theory of relativity. (I am not sure that it is an even dozen, since I have not met the other eleven! But I am sure there must be at least twelve.)

In the history of humanity, no mind has ever mastered the mystery of the Trinity. Although the fact of God can be comprehended by human wisdom, it was not invented by human reason. Conceding, then, that there is a God Whose powers exceed human thinking, we stand on the threshold of a proper approach to a study of the miracles.

In the text that we have cited, three things are stated about miracles that should bound the horizon of our thinking. The first statement is that there were miracles: "This beginning of miracles did Jesus in Cana of Galilee." The word "beginning" implies continuity. There were others that followed, until the date of termination of miracles, or else the word "beginning" is out of place. This is a frank and bold statement that miracles did occur in connection with the ministry of the Son of God.

We would suggest that most of our misunderstanding springs from a wrong approach to this study. There are two ways through which we may seek understanding of the

miraculous. The first is the wrong way, but it is the one
most commonly employed—that is, to seek to understand
the fact involved in the miracle.

No human being can add to our argument in this sphere
by attempting to master the fact involved in the perform-
ance of miracles. We read in Acts 26:8 that Paul addressed
a question to Agrippa: "Why should it be thought a thing
incredible with you, that God should raise the dead?" The
answer depends upon the point of emphasis. If Paul said
to King Agrippa, "Why should it be accounted a thing incredible with thee that God *should raise the dead?*" the
answer would be immediate. To a Roman, the fact of a
resurrection would not only be incredible but fantastic.
This was contrary to all Roman experience. They knew
that when they buried their dead, they stayed dead, and
that seemed to be the end of them. But if Paul had placed
the emphasis upon the person concerned, we would have
a totally different approach. Suppose he said, "Why should
it be counted a thing incredible with thee that *God* should
raise the dead?" A new issue is at once implied. Granted
the fact of God, we must then concede that nothing is impossible if He desires to do it.

To come back to the context in the second chapter of
John, we must admit at once that we have no possible idea
as to how water was turned into wine. But ignorance in
this sphere need not concern us, since we definitely, do
know *Who* turned water into wine. In a word, then, the
problem of understanding miracles is to be approached in
the light of the Person involved.

The second statement in our text conveys the idea of the
purpose of miracles. "This beginning of miracles did
Jesus in Cana of Galilee, and manifested forth His glory."
Miracles were for the definite purpose of demonstrating

the supernatural nature of the man Christ Jesus. For the same reason that a bird sings or a dog barks, God works wonders beyond the comprehension of man. If Jesus Christ was the son of God, the supernatural was natural to Him.

Herein lies the answer to those who ask, "Why are we not seeing miracles in our day and age?" The first rule for viewing a miracle is that you must be there when the miracle occurs. If Jesus Christ were walking the earth today, miracles would again be common. In the day of His earthly reign, the things that we now term miraculous had become part of the ordinary business of living because of the release of His power due to His physical presence.

Nor does it avail to doubt and to say, "I never saw a miracle." *Greenleaf on Evidence* states "the court cannot permit clear and unmistakable testimony to be set aside on the basis of the lack of experience of the objector." If ten thousand people would take the witness stand and say, "I never saw a miracle," this would not be sufficient to overturn the word of Matthew, Luke, and John, who can say, "I did see a miracle." The testimony of two or three witnesses who were present when an event occurred is more conclusive under the rigid demands of the laws of evidence than the testimony of a million persons who were nowhere near the scene when the event transpired.

So when the Son of God did walk the earth in the flesh of a man, it was natural that miracles should accompany His appearance to manifest His glory.

Our text then concludes by defining the result of miracles: "And His disciples believed on Him." The miraculous events that are set forth in the Scriptures are put there to convert the doubting and the skeptical. They were additional evidence to strengthen the faith of those who believed on

Him and to give them more reason for the hope that is in their hearts. To show exactly what we mean, we need only point out that no man who really believes in Jesus Christ doubts for a single minute that He did work miracles as the Word of God clearly states. This is an unanswerable reason to the believer. When we have been close enough to Calvary so the grace of the Lord Jesus Christ results in our own regeneration, the miracle of this new birth is so stupendous that we have no difficulty in believing the lesser miracles, such as the turning of water into wine! If the word of life that was manifested in Jesus Christ can transmute a sinner into a saint, why could not the same power change the nature of one fluid into something closely similar? Wine naturally comes from water through the medium of the vine. On the contrary, saints do not naturally come from sinners. There is no known process of development by which the lecherous, alien nature of man can naturally and normally develop into a child of God. Therefore, we are reluctantly forced to the conclusion that those who doubt the miracles have never experienced the great miracle of the new birth. It is, then, useless to argue with them, for they have no ground of common understanding.

We then return to our original premise. We should heartily suggest to those who desire an understanding of miracles in the Word of God to discontinue their fruitless practice of seeking to understand the fact involved. Turn all your attention to the Person Whose power is manifested in these supernatural works and understanding and belief will bring comfort and peace to your heart.

INVESTING FOR PROFIT

WE ARE CHANGED

But we all, with open face beholding as in a glass the glory of the Lord, are changed into the same image from glory to glory, even as by the Spirit of the Lord. — II Cor. 3:18

You are all acquainted with Hawthorne's story of the "Great Stone Face." Here was a man who had throughout his entire life lived in sight of the Great Stone Face and had spent hours untold contemplating it and admiring it. Finally his friends and neighbors awoke to the realization that he had come to resemble the great face of the mountain. Just a story, of course, but I believe that it contains a tremendous truth. That is why the Psalmist says in the Twenty-seventh Psalm: "One thing have I desired of the Lord, that will I seek after; that I may dwell in the house of the Lord all the days of my life, to behold the beauty of the Lord, and to enquire in His temple."

Remember the vital importance of allowing nothing to operate upon your life by your consent that does not make you more like Christ. Determine now that you will give your full consent always to God as He deals with you by His Spirit.

Dr. Stephen W. Paine,
President, Houghton College.

INVESTING FOR PROFIT

By Dr. Charles W. Koller, Th. D.
President, Northern Baptist Theological Seminary

SOME YEARS AGO a leading life insurance company undertook to find the cost of rearing a child from infancy through high school graduation. After long and careful research, it was concluded that the average cost of rearing an American boy is $6,077. In the case of a girl, it is $90 more. Presumably that $90 is justified on the assumption that the girl is worth more. In any event, the cost in dollars and cents is no small matter.

Yet the financial cost is by far the smallest item that enters into the rearing of a boy or a girl. There must be added the immeasurable cost in time, labor, tears, and prayers incident to the rearing of a boy or girl. There are those long, sleepless nights, those innumerable childhood ailments, the vexing disciplinary problems, and a thousand other items that can be understood and appreciated only by the parent who has reared a child. To all of this we must add the labors of teachers, pastors, and others who have made their contribution to the intellectual and spiritual training of the child. But all of this is as nothing compared with the infinite measure of divine resources the heavenly Father has poured into every life. All things considered, the cost of a young man or a young woman in college is overwhelming.

What shall we do with this complex treasure that has been entrusted to us? The youth cannot redistribute himself to the sources from which he came, but he casts the deciding vote as to what shall become of that treasure. How will he invest his life to insure the largest measure of returns upon the investment? Where will he invest so as to insure the largest possible measure of happiness to himself, and blessing to the world, and satisfaction to the God Who created him? The principles of profitable investment in the commercial world are similarly valid in the investment of a life.

I. *To insure the largest possible yield, we must invest early.*

A treasure of ten thousand dollars invested at the age of seventeen and compounded at prevailing rates of interest would grow to about a quarter of a million by the age of seventy. Left uninvested, it remains without increase. A life placed early under the leading and care and blessing of God will yield rich, lifelong dividends. The longer we wait, the smaller the profit. A man who died at the age of ninety-one remarked with deep fervor and earnestness shortly before his death that he had yielded himself to the Lord at the age of eighty-nine, and that the last two years of his life, in spite of weakness and continuous suffering, were by far the happiest years of his whole life. Having contracted an incurable internal cancer, he had been unable to sleep, and it was in those long, sleepless nights that he began to think about God and ultimately yielded his soul to the Savior. The regret of which he often spoke with tears was that he had not yielded himself to his Lord in early life.

Two brothers who were reared in the same home came to the parting of the ways when they were about twelve years old. They had been taught by the same Sunday-school teachers and the same pastors; now in a series of evangelistic meetings they had, night after night, listened to the same preacher and felt the same tug of the Holy Spirit within their hearts. The one yielded, and God took charge of his life. He grew in spiritual stature and in favor with God and man. In the Lord's leading, he became in time one of the most famous and most fruitful missionaries that has ever blessed the world. Thousands were brought into the kingdom of Christ through his ministry. His brother, resisting the Holy Spirit, went on through life without yielding himself to the Lord. Finally, when he was over eighty years old, he gave himself to the Lord. He was so enfeebled with the infirmities of old age that it required four men to baptize him. The short time that remained until his death was bright with the radiance of heaven, but the long, meager, wasted years that had gone before could not be restored.

The extraordinary blessedness described in the First Psalm is pronounced upon him who "walketh not in the counsel of the ungodly, nor standeth in the way of sinners, nor sitteth in the seat of the scornful." Hebrew scholars tell us that the language in the original might be more accurately translated, "Blessed is the man who *never did* walk . . . stand . . . sit . . ." By so much as he has drifted into unwholesome associations and practices, his blessedness and fruitfulness have been reduced. It is significant that the Word of God pronounces a special measure of blessing upon those who "have not known the depths of Satan." There is knowledge that impoverishes life. One of the blessings of an early yielding to the Savior is that the life is kept free from devastating knowledge and experiences.

II. *To insure the largest possible yield, we must invest carefully.*

There must be a right purpose in life. A certain prosperous farmer was asked what he was going to do with his enormous corn crop. He replied that he would buy hogs and fatten them for the market. Then, being asked what he would do with the profits, he replied that he would buy more land. In answer to the question—"What would you do then?" he replied that he would raise more corn. After that he would buy more hogs and market them and afterwards buy more land. More corn—more hogs—more land! And so the cycle goes on repeating itself without purpose or objective. The aimless philosophy of that farmer has its counterpart in many a life.

Besides a worthy purpose, the youth needs to be careful, also, as to the place where he invests his life. Nothing will bring failure more surely than to devote oneself to the wrong calling. The disciples were called of Christ to become fishers of men. After that there was no success for them in the other kind of fishing. Becoming discouraged, they apparently were abandoning the ministry of the gospel and returning to their nets and fishes. Here the Lord Jesus found them after His resurrection. They had fished all night in utter failure. It was only as the Lord Jesus graciously identified Himself with their labors that success returned (John 21:6). Jesus commanded them to cast the net "on the right side of the boat." As a matter of fact, that was what they had been trying to do all night, but only Jesus knew which was the right side of the boat. What they needed was the direction of Jesus. Without Him, they had been missing success by the breadth of a boat.

The long breakwater of huge rocks outside the seawall at Galveston is said to have cost fourteen million dollars. Some of the citizens remarked that they would not permit it to be removed for fifty million dollars. Those rocks have no particular comeliness from any possible point of view. In certain areas, whole mountain ranges of better looking rocks can be found, which are not worth fourteen cents in the aggregate. It is altogether a matter of place. A human life rightly placed may be of immeasurable value. The same life in the wrong place and calling may be a total loss.

III. *To insure the largest possible yield, we must invest liberally.*

A man with a huge capital to invest would be very foolish investing only a small portion of it and foregoing the possible profit on the remainder. And yet this is what many a Christian is doing—yielding only a portion of himself to the service of Christ. We cannot with-hold a part of our time, talents, and resources from the service of Christ and still have the full blessing. This is the emphasis in Rom. 12:1-2, where we are bidden to yield ourselves bodily to the Lord. If we do less than to yield ourselves bodily, we are going to have less than the full blessing. This Scripture sets forth the one condition upon which we may know the "perfect" will of God. With less than the full measure of consecration here required, we not only fail to attain to the perfect will of God; we fail even to know what that perfect will is, and all that we can hope for is God's second best or less.

The rich young ruler was willing to go a part of the way with Christ, but refusing to yield himself bodily, he lost the blessing and "went away sorrowful." In contrast, we see those fully consecrated disciples at Pentecost, who had yielded everything to Christ and yet "did eat their meat with gladness and singleness of heart, praising God and having favor with all the people." Theirs was a perfect case of profitable investment with a perfect result!

A BURDEN OF PRAYER
FOR DR. CHOW

FORGETTING THOSE THINGS WHICH ARE BEHIND

There is today much of the drifting attitude of going where the wind blows. We need Christians with a forward look, Christians who know what they believe and who live it.

Moses had a real devotion to his task. When Pharaoh could not argue any longer with him, he asked Moses how many were going. Moses replied, "We are all going. Not one hoof will we leave behind."

Jeremiah and John both had it. There were failures, of course, as Demas. But you will never fail if you give yourself wholeheartedly to the task.

The poor Apostle Paul would have sunk if he had not been able to forget his past. Not a man in the world has the right to forget the past except the believer. The unsaved man will meet his past when he gives an account of every ungodly thing he has done or spoken. But the Apostle Paul had a past that was forgiven. God had set him free; He had justified him.

So we, too, as believers, may forget the past and devote ourselves today to the things of Christ.

THE REV. DAVID JOHNSON,
of Chicago.

A BURDEN OF PRAYER FOR DR. CHOW

By Dr. James R. Graham, Jr., D.D.
Special Lecturer in Bible, Wheaton College

I was preaching in Wuchang, one of the twin cities of central China. I noticed a well-dressed man sitting in the rear of the church. He looked rather bored. Seated in a pew all by himself, he put his foot up on the bench, braced his back in the corner of the pew, and tried to settle down for a comfortable nap.

Presently I began to read from the Mandarin Bible. The passage was Matthew 24. The man in the rear of the hall began to prick up his ears just a wee bit and to evince some interest that a foreigner could read the Mandarin with a rather unusual degree of facility. Having read a portion of the great Olivet discourse containing the signs of the age as given by the Savior Himself, I proceeded to give a message on the signs of the second advent of Christ, citing recent world conditions and international relationships, the general breakdown of morals, the departure from revealed truth as fulfillments of the sign. The man on the back seat was unable to go through with his nap. In spite of himself, be became deeply interested, straightened up his back, put both feet on the floor, and then leaned over on the seat in front with arms folded and chin on the back of his hands. His eyes burned into me as I set forth the truth of the near return in judgment of the Son of God.

After the service was over, he came down to the front to speak to me. Rarely have I seen such agitation. Sputtering in alternate English and Chinese, he began to shout, "It's true. It's true. Every word that you say is true. I never knew that these things were revealed in the Bible. May I go with you to your house and talk with you further concerning these matters?" I readily agreed.

As we walked along to the house, I learned that he was the dean of the Science Department of a great university there in Wuchang, a Doctor of Philosophy from one of our American universities. We had a long and earnest conversation, and my friend, Dr. Chung, really met the Lord Jesus. A fire was kindled within him the like of which I have never encountered before in a spiritual babe.

At the next few meetings he was present, each time with his Bible open, listening with avid interest. On Saturday evening, he told me about a certain friend whom he had brought in as a professor of mathematics in his department. His friend was in Shanghai in a hospital and felt he was going to die shortly from a serious kidney malady. As he told me about it, he showed the greatest agitation, and shouted, "He is going to hell."

The next morning I looked for the doctor in the morning service. I scanned the audience in vain for his shining countenance. He didn't appear, but attended the afternoon service, seemingly more eager than ever. Following the afternoon service, he again came to have a conversation with me.

"You may have noticed," he said, "that I was absent from the morning service."

I assured him that I had taken note of it. He said, "I had my Bible in hand and was going out the door of my house in Hankow (Hankow is across the Yangtze River from Wuchang), but as I started out the door, it seemed as if some unseen force literally thrust me down upon the floor in a passion of prayer for the salvation of Dr. Chow (the mathematics professor of whom he had spoken the day before). I had hardly been able to sleep all of Saturday night, thinking of my friend's near approach to eternity without Christ. So when this overpowering burden of prayer came upon me, I knelt there on the floor of my own room and cried aloud to God, literally weeping a puddle of tears. The paroxysm of agony continued for about an hour. Then as suddenly as it came, it departed, and I rose from my knees with absolute peace of heart and mind. Looking at the clock, I saw that it was 11:30 and realized that it was too late for me now to arrive at the morning service. So I decided simply to stay at home until time to leave for the afternoon service.

"Now, Brother Graham, what I want to see you about is to exact a promise from you that as soon as you are able to return down the river, you will go to Shanghai and call on this friend of mine whose life hangs in the balance and minister Christ to him before he goes hence."

I promised him that I would do this at my own earliest convenience, and that if I were delayed, I would communicate with some other Christian in Shanghai to go and perform this ministry. That night at the conclusion of the meetings, I took a ship down the river to my home near Nanking, and after a few days of Bible conference in my own town of Chinkiang, I boarded a train and went to Shanghai. I knew a wonderful Christian missionary doctor who worked there, the beloved Dr. Thornton Stearns. Upon my arrival in Shanghai, I called Dr. Stearns over the phone and made a date with him to go to the bedside of the mathematics professor. Promptly at 9 o'clock the following morning, my friend met me on the steps of the hospital. We went into the hospital office of the registrar to seek information as to the room in which Dr. Chow would be located (the Red Cross Hospital of Shanghai has about four hundred beds). As the registrar began to thumb through his records for the name, another young clerk came in and courteously asked me whom I sought. I told him Dr. Chow Chia-Su. He replied with a very solemn face and a shake of the head:

"Dr. Chow Chia-Su has left the earth."

About that time the registrar came across the record and nodded agreement with what his colleague had told me, producing a yellow hospital record sheet, at which I directed an amateur and Dr. Stearns a professional glance. There was a signed statement by the attending physician that Dr. Chow had left this life, but the thing that attracted my attention was the date and the time. It was on February 9 at 11:30 A. M. When I first heard that our mathematics professor had passed away, I wondered for just a moment why the Lord had brought me there after the death had already occurred. But as soon as I saw the date and the time, I told Dr. Stearns, "I know now that you and I have missed seeing him, but we shall meet the mathematics professor one day in the glory."

My friend asked me how I arrived at that conclusion. I told him that the Lord never lays a burden of prayer such as was described to me by Dr. Chung of Hankow, without intending to answer such prayer. The fact that the passing of Dr. Chow exactly coincided with the time that Dr. Chung had arisen from his knees and was relieved of his burden, gave double assurance that the prayer was in the Holy Spirit.

I bade my friend, Dr. Stearns, good-by and got on the train and returned to my home, content to let the divine principle illustrated in this connection wait for eternity for its vindication. In the council of God, I was not required to wait that long. Only a few days afterward, I was asked to speak at a mission high school for girls in my own city. The text that morning was from the Ninetieth Psalm, "So teach us to number our days that we may apply our hearts unto wisdom." I completed the message with the story of the Chinese educator in Wuchang whose heart had become aflame with the love of Christ and who had called upon God with strong crying and tears to save his friend. At the end of the story, I told them I felt today, due to the prayer of this friend, we should all have the pleasure of seeing Dr. Chow Chia-Su in the glory one day. As the name of the mathematics professor slipped from my mouth, I noticed that there were signs of recognition in the audience of girls. I thought that was not surprising since he was a very eminent scholar and well known in Nanking and all through the Yangtze Valley.

After the prayer of dismissal, the Chinese lady principal of the high school asked me if I would wait for her a moment in her office. She had a word to speak to me. This I agreed to do, and when she came in, she sat down on the other side of the desk from me and said, "Mr. Graham, that is a very interesting story that you told at the last of your message this morning. The most interesting part of it is that I know the other half of it. The gentleman to whom you referred, who has now passed away, is a son-in-law of this school. His wife is an alumna and incidentally a former principal, a graduate of Columbia University of New York. Her name is Ai loa. Just a few days ago she came into this very office to see me. I had not seen her for sometime and I had heard the report that her husband was dead. I found it difficult, therefore, to explain the fact of her peace and joy of countenance when she came in, coupled with the fact that she had on no widows' weeds or anything of that nature. I thought I must have been mistaken about her husband's death else she could not have appeared so neat.

"After we had exchanged greetings, I said, 'And how is your husband? I heard that he was sick.' 'Oh, yes,' she replied; 'he is gone to be with Jesus, and I shall meet him in His presence one day.' "

"I was very much amazed at this statement," went on the lady principal, "because this couple were rather notoriously irreligious in our set, and how she could speak so confidently that her husband had gone to be with Jesus and that she would meet him there one day amazed me beyond words. So I asked her for the basis of her assurance.

"She replied, 'It is all very wonderful. I can't even explain it myself. My husband was at the point of death; we all knew the end was near. He had been unconscious or in a coma all of that Sunday morning. At about 10:30, as several of us stood around the room, he raised his head up off his pillow and with a very clear eye and voice, declared to us all that he had seen Jesus Christ nailed on the cross for his sins. "I do not know why," he said; "the conviction has become so plain to me, but I know that He died for me. I know that I believe in Him. I know that I have eternal life and that I shall enter shortly into His presence. My dear wife," he said, addressing me, "we have wasted our lives. We have known of this gospel. We have neglected it. I urge you here and now, before I go hence, to trust Jesus Christ for salvation and to give your life to make Him known. In the school that we own and operate in Nanking, see to it that you have true Christian ministers to come there and preach the gospel to our students from now on." After so charging us, he put his head back on the pillow and his lips began to move and we could hear presently the tones of a gospel song that he had learned long ago but which I had never heard him sing. We were amazed at the strength and clarity of his voice, and when the song was over, in clear, audible tones, drawing it from somewhere in the long hidden archives of his memory, there came forth from beginning to end the love chapter (I Corinthians 13). He ended up, "and now abideth faith, hope, love, these three, but the greatest of these is love." And as he spoke these words, his spirit fled from his body and he was drawn into the presence of the Savior whom he had so recently trusted.'

"So, Mr. Graham," went on the lady principal, "your judgment is correct. We shall see Dr. Chow one day in the glory."

It is strange how astonished we can be at that which we even claim to expect. My heart was filled with a song. I never reached the bedside of Dr. Chow in time, but the Holy Spirit, the Teacher, the Regenerator, the One who leads men to Christ, preceded me and did a much better work than I could have done. It happened that a few days later it was my pleasure to see the lovely wife of the deceased mathematics professor and to hear from her lips the testimony of God's grace to her husband and to herself and to her husband's brother, all because of the effectual fervent prayer of a friend whose heart was aflame with the love of Christ.

DATE DUE

MAR 6 1980			